Project Bloom

A Yogi's Wisdom for the Workplace

By
Kevin Wilson

Equinox One Publishing

This book is based on true events, although, some names have been changed. Any resemblance to real people, living or dead, is entirely coincidental.

Cover Design by Shoma Joshi and Melissa Paige Taylor
Editorial by Claire Smith and Jennifer Wauson

Equinox **One**
Publishing

www.Equinoxonepublishing.com

ISBN-13: 978-0615638072 (Equinox One Publishing)
ISBN-10: 0615638074

Contents

1

Before Meets After

Not too long ago, a day-trader who had traded himself into bankruptcy went into the offices of the day-trading firm and killed nine people and wounded twelve. I have often wondered how someone could get his life and work tangled into such a mess that he would turn to this kind of violence as a way to solve his problems. Maybe he was bullied and harassed by his coworkers to the point that he couldn't take it anymore. Perhaps he had been fired unjustly, so he sought revenge on a former boss. Maybe he was passed over for a raise or promotion, or been demoted or disciplined in some way that felt unfair. Whatever the reason, I could only imagine the killer felt that he was the victim, and violence was the only way to settle the score.

The killings at the day-trading firm happened not too far from my office. After the shooting, the killer fled the scene, and no one was quite sure where he was going next. The security guards in my building received word of the shooting and decided to secure our building to keep anyone from entering or leaving.

Sitting at my desk that afternoon in my office in the human resources department, I came up with another theory about workplace violence. Maybe sometimes it's the little things that cause these incidents: stress, deadlines, disrespect, turf wars, and corporate backstabbing. Throw these ingredients into the pressure cooker, and a simple, single negative comment could be the last straw that causes a steaming, violent eruption. Of course, there is no justification for violence, but what it really comes down to is that someone didn't get what he wanted.

Let's face it, everyone gets angry. Most of the time, we do a good job of suppressing that little monster that always wants its way. But admit it. There are times when you harbor negative thoughts toward your boss, a family member, neighbor, or a rude motorist on the highway. Most of the time, we grit our teeth and don't take action, but the thoughts are there nonetheless.

I used to have feelings like this from time to time. Frustrating things would happen in my life that caused me to react rather than take time to respond. As this occurred day after day, anger would build up inside me, and I would end up taking it out on some innocent third party such as my wife. I never got to the point that I grabbed a gun and went after my coworkers like the guy at the day-trading firm, but I was still an emotional accident waiting to happen.

What probably saved everyone from suffering my emotional wrath is that I learned to meditate. Once I learned a simple practice that I could do by myself every day, my anger subsided and my emotions were once again under my control. My life was transformed in the process, and I was amazed at how it changed my life. My meditation practice not only improved my personal life, it also became an essential business tool that boosted my career.

One example of how meditation changed my work-life is reflected in the name of this book, Project Bloom. The afternoon the day-trader went mad and our building was locked down was also the magical beginning for Project Bloom. I stayed late that evening to avoid the traffic and wrote a proposal for a unique diversity program with a goal of improving the wellbeing of the people who worked in my department.

If you had worked in our office with me before Project Bloom, you wouldn't recognize the place afterward. Before, we didn't socialize much with each other. Each person just did his or her job and nothing extra. We didn't go out of our way to help each other, and there was a lot of resistance to change. The departments within human resources avoided interaction with the other departments as much as possible, didn't trust each other, and blamed each other when things went wrong, which made the word "teamwork" meaningless.

Project Bloom transformed our workplace. After we implemented Project Bloom, we worked together like a close-knit family. We cared about each other, we communicated better, we appreciated and recognized each other, and we took time to develop ourselves. I don't have statistics that show the impact Project Bloom had on productivity or employee retention, but I can tell you that after we implemented Project Bloom, our department was a great place to work, and everyone benefited.

The inspiration for Project Bloom was a direct result of my meditation practice. One day after finishing my meditation in my office, the idea for the program just popped into my mind—already fully formed and well-thought out. Interestingly, this is a phenomenon that is a common side effect of meditation. One's innate, nonlogical intelligence begins to bloom, one's clarity of understanding improves dramatically, and the accuracy of one's decision-making skills increases.

The seed for Project Bloom was planted by the man who taught me how to meditate, Sadhguru Jaggi Vasudev. Sadhguru is a world-renowned yogi from India who is also the founder of Isha Foundation, a volunteer-run, international nonprofit organization dedicated to cultivating human potential. Sadhguru is based in southern India, but he teaches yoga and meditation classes around the world. He has offered programs at companies like Ford Motor Company and Microsoft to prisons filled with hardened criminals. If you look on Isha Foundation's website at www.ishafoundation.org, you will see that Sadhguru is described as a visionary humanitarian and prominent spiritual leader who works tirelessly toward the physical, mental, and spiritual wellbeing of everyone. I can tell you from personal experience that every word of that is true. I have never met anyone so selfless, with so much compassion, who is completely dedicated to helping others bloom.

Named one of India's fifty most influential people, Sadhguru has spoken at some of the world's most prominent international leadership forums. He participated in numerous panels at the World Economic Forum and spoke on issues ranging from diplomacy and economic development to education and the environment. He has addressed the Tällberg Forum in Sweden, the Australian Leadership Retreat, and served as a delegate to the United Nations Millennium Peace Summit and the World Peace Congress.

I met Sadhguru when he visited my city and taught a yoga and meditation class. During the class, Sadhguru introduced the concept of "inner management," the idea that people must first be able to manage themselves before they attempt to manage others. To me, this was an obvious truth that was often ignored in business. When I heard Sadhguru talk about inner management, I thought about its application in business, and I wanted to know how meditation could impact the workplace.

About six months after learning to meditate, I made arrangements to meet with Sadhguru the next time he visited the United States. When we met and began talking, I explained that I wanted to explore the impact of meditation in the workplace.

"People forget that the fundamental purpose of business is human wellbeing," Sadhguru replied. "Anything that improves human wellbeing is relevant to business."

The organization that Sadhguru runs, Isha Foundation, is proof that he knows how to motivate and manage people. Throughout southern India, Isha Foundation operates over a dozen mobile medical trucks that provide free health care to several hundred thousand rural village people. The organization also builds and runs schools and computer labs for poor children, organizes massive tree planting efforts, and teaches yoga and meditation classes, all of which are accomplished on a nonprofit basis by unpaid volunteers.

During my meeting with Sadhguru, I proposed that we organize a business roundtable and invite various business people to meet with him to explore his ideas on management and leadership. Sadhguru agreed to participate during his next visit to the United States.

That business roundtable was truly one of the most inspirational business meetings I had ever attended. Sadhguru's ideas on leadership, engagement, career development, and the importance of meditation in business inspired me to start Project Bloom to test his concepts and see what kind of impact they would have. I'm happy to say that our experiment was incredibly successful. As a result, we decided to share what we discussed during the business roundtable in this book so that other organizations might also benefit. With interviews from business people who insist that meditation is an essential business tool, practical advice from Sadhguru on how to enhance your career, and blueprints for projects that can transform your workplace, you'll learn about the value meditation can have in your own life. While you can't effectively learn meditation from a book, there are various online resources that offer several options for meditation training that anyone can do at home. I hope that you'll give them a try and see for yourself what meditation can do for your own career.

2

Success at Any Cost

In the four months that passed before Sadhguru's next visit, I gathered a group of business people together, and we formulated questions for the roundtable meeting with Sadhguru.

Among those invited was a woman named Raquel, a long-time friend and associate who ran her own consulting business along with her husband. She managed a team of twelve other consultants who worked for companies all over the world. Primarily, they represented companies at trade shows, made presentations to convention audiences, and helped coach field salespeople. Raquel had heard my wife, Jennifer, and me talk about Sadhguru numerous times, but she had never met him.

Kyle was another friend I had met when we worked together at IBM. Kyle had just been promoted to manager in an IT department for another company, so he was eager to get management and leadership advice. Like Raquel, Kyle knew a little about Sadhguru, but he had never met him.

Another attendee was a fifty-year-old, gray-haired man named Robert, an executive director who had managed a team of salespeople and worked for a large Fortune 50 company. He had never heard of Sadhguru but was intrigued enough at the prospect of talking face-to-face with a yogi from India that he blocked off his afternoon so he could attend.

A number of other business people were invited to give us a total of fifteen members for the roundtable. Of those, a cross section of managers, business owners, and rank-and-file employees were there. Thus, ours was a diverse range of perspectives regarding the challenges of the workplace.

The day we had scheduled for the business roundtable coincided with a yoga and meditation class Sadhguru was teaching that evening. To save time, we used the same conference center that had been secured for the class. We sat up the tables and chairs for the roundtable in one of the meeting rooms next to the ballroom where 250 people would later attend the class.

Around 9:00 a.m., I went to pick up Sadhguru from the corporate condo where he was staying. When I arrived at the gate, I called the phone number I had been given and was buzzed into the maze of gated-community streets.

I parked my van in front of Sadhguru's condo, got out, and rang the doorbell. Sadhguru's assistant, Leela, greeted me at the door. Leela led me into the living room, where I sat on the sofa. She then excused herself into the kitchen, where she was in the middle of cooking something for breakfast.

I was looking at the laptop that was set up on the table in front of me, when Sadhguru entered the room. I was impressed by how distinguished he looked; his dark brown face was highlighted by his white hair and full beard, and he wore a textured brown shawl draped over his right shoulder. On his head was a burnt orange turban.

"Hello, Kevin," he said. "Would you like something to eat?"

"No, thank you," I responded, somewhat surprised at the invitation. "I've eaten already."

Sadhguru then sat at the dining room table, and Leela soon brought him something that looked like a potato pancake and some fruit. They talked with each other for a moment in Tamil, the language of southern India, and then Sadhguru began to eat.

I grabbed an apartment locator magazine on the end table and began flipping through the pages, but my eyes weren't really seeing the apartments pictured in the glossy publication. Instead, I was thinking about what an incredible opportunity lay before me.

"So, we are going to talk about business today?" Sadhguru suddenly asked from the dining room between bites.

"Yes," I said enthusiastically. "I have a long list of questions."

"What kind of questions?"

"Well, I know we won't get to everything on my list," I explained, "but, I'm interested in how meditation can affect the workplace. I have questions about work-life balance, management, leadership, stress management—"

"Stress management?" Sadhguru interrupted me with a smile. "When I first landed in the United States a few years ago, I kept hearing this stress management everywhere. I could not understand why anybody would manage their stress. I can understand you want to manage your money, your business, your family, your property. But why would anybody want to manage their stress? It took me a while to understand that you have established a whole culture of believing that stress is a part of your life. Stress is not a part of your life. It is not the nature of the work that you are doing which is causing stress; it is just that you have no control over your systems."

Sadhguru continued eating, and after a few more bites asked, "Who will be there?"

"Business people with different backgrounds," I answered. "A few CEOs, vice presidents, directors, managers, small business owners, and general employees."

Sadhguru nodded and then continued eating. There was a long period of silence, so I turned back to the apartment locator magazine.

"Are you thinking about moving?" he asked with a smile, noticing my fake interest in the magazine.

"No," I laughed. "Just something to look at while I'm waiting." I put the magazine down and looked around the room and finally out the window.

About that time, Sadhguru finished eating and got up from the table. "I'm ready," he said, gesturing with outstretched arms. "Let's go!"

We left the apartment together, got in my van, and I drove him to the conference center that was located about fifteen minutes away.

My wife, Jennifer, who had previously attended one of Sadhguru's meditation workshops, is also a documentary producer and director. She had arranged to videotape the talk, so the conference room was filled with cameras, tripods, and light stands, including several lights hanging from the ceiling. Everything in the room was focused on Sadhguru as he sat down in his chair and tucked one of his legs up under the other.

"What shall we talk about?" Sadhguru asked the audience to begin the discussion.

Raquel asked the first question. "My question is this, Sadhguru," Raquel began. "I work all the time, and I have a very successful career and business. This is what I thought I always wanted, but something seems to be missing. I never seem to stay satisfied. I'm not happy. I get frustrated a lot. What am I doing wrong?"

"This is an endemic problem around the world," Sadhguru said with a laugh. "You go to the people who are doing top-level managerial jobs, or you go to the lowest person on the corporate ladder; everybody feels somewhere it is their

bbing them of their happiness. But would you be happy if you

ooked at Raquel and waited for a response.

_el answered.

"So, it is not the work which is taking away your happiness," Sadhguru continued. "If you did not have a job, you would not be happy. If you have a job, you will not be happy. If you are not too busy, you will not be happy. If you get very busy, you are not happy. So the issue is not at all about work. Work is just an excuse for your unhappiness. If a human being is not happy, you need to look at it in a much more basic way."

Raquel nodded slowly.

Sadhguru cleared his throat and then looked back at Raquel. "If you look at all the activity that you are doing in your life, all the activity that every human being is pursuing in his life, actually everything is being done in pursuit of happiness. Everything that we do—whether we pursue education or we build businesses, or families, or pursue careers—whatever we are doing, we are in pursuit of happiness. But in this pursuit of happiness, it looks like we are losing happiness rather than gaining happiness."

"How do we get it back?" Raquel asked.

"I think you are successful enough to understand, in your outside lives, that with the outside situations, unless you do the right thing, it won't work. The same goes for the inner situation also, because happiness is an inner situation. Whenever you are happy, it blossoms from within and finds an external expression. But right now, somehow, we have mortgaged this to an outside situation."

"Are you saying that we're waiting for something else to make us happy," Raquel continued, "rather than just *being* happy?"

Sadhguru looked at her and nodded. "The happiness is within," he explained, "but we have kept the stimulus outside, or, in other words, it's like this: if you owned a car in 1920s, when you buy a car, along with it you have to get yourself two servants because in the morning you have to push-start the car. Later, probably in '40s if you bought a car, you had to get yourself one servant because it's a crank-start. But today all your cars are self-start. It's time you put your happiness on self-start. And anyways, no one is willing to be your servant anymore."

Sadhguru laughed, which helped ease the tension Raquel was obviously feeling.

"I still have a car like that," Raquel laughed. "It always needs a jump-start."

"Your family situation, or work situation, or the situation in the world need not jump-start your happiness," Sadhguru explained. "If you know how to start your happiness by yourself, if you understand the dynamics of what this human being is, how she functions, then being peaceful and happy would come naturally to you—"

"It does," Raquel interrupted, "some of the time. But there are a lot of ups and downs in my business, and the downtimes get me down."

"Now, when you are running your business, are you not looking at all the dynamics of how to make this happen? Otherwise, would you still be successful? If you are successful without looking at anything carefully, you are just successful by accident, not by intent. When you are successful by accident, then you will be anxious all the time. That is so with the outside situation; that is so with the inside situation. So right now, your peace and happiness is happening by accident. Once in a while when outside situations come together, you are happy.

"This is one thing that you must understand, you will never have situations in such a way that one hundred percent the way you want it. Nobody in the world has situations that way. Outside situations are always happening to some extent the way we want it, and the rest of it is not happening the way we want it. That is always the reality. Even if there are just two people in the family, it does not go exactly the way you want it, and it should not. Because if everything goes the way *you* want it, where will *I* go? Where will your husband go? Where will everybody else in the world go?"

Everyone laughed, including Raquel. "I get the point," Raquel said a bit sheepishly.

"As the scope and play of your life becomes bigger and bigger, less and less will be under your control. Now all the time you are longing to expand the scope and play of your life; at the same time whenever things don't go the way you think it should go, then you are getting distressed."

"You're right," Raquel said. "That's my life, exactly."

Sadhguru looked at Raquel and smiled compassionately. "If the process of work has led you to a point of distress in your life, it's time you looked inward to see what you can do about your interiority. As there is a technology to create outside situations the way we want it, to engineer the world the way we want it or the way we feel is convenient and comfortable for us, accordingly there is a technology and a science to create an inner situation the way you want it.

"So if you had the choice of creating an inner situation the way you want it, obviously you would make sure that you're joyful and peaceful. Isn't it so?" Sadhguru asked.

"Of course," Raquel responded.

"Right now, you are unable to consciously create an inner situation the way you want it," Sadhguru explained. "So happiness and satisfaction are not going to happen because you reach somewhere in your job. If you create the fundamental format of happiness within you, then you function at your optimal level. This way you will be successful. You will then see that your mind, your emotion, your intelligence, everything functions at its best.

"Once, a business executive went into the country," Sadhguru began. "And he stayed in a country home, woke up, and came out, and there was a shepherd in the garden. He asked the shepherd, 'What's the weather going to be like?' The shepherd said, 'Today's weather is going to be the kind of weather that I like very much.' 'What kind of weather do you like?,' asked the executive. Then the shepherd said, 'Whatever kind of weather there is today, I like that kind of weather. Because I have understood from my experience with nature, you can't decide how the weather should be. And so I have learned to like whatever kind of weather there is today. So today definitely is going to be the kind of weather that I like.'"

Sadhguru laughed heartily, which brought a smile to Raquel's face.

I decided to take some notes, and grabbed my pen and started writing furiously in my notebook. I scribbled, *Regardless of the weather outside today, you are responsible for the weather inside yourself.* I then thought about all the meaningless small talk with business associates in the hall about how the weather was today. "That rain is really going to make a mess of the commute," someone might say. But what did it really matter how the weather was today? What really mattered was what was going on inside a person. Wouldn't it be great to work with people who exuded a warm spring day? If the people with whom you worked could only control the weather inside themselves, what a pleasant experience work could be.

3

Enough Is Enough

As I listened to Sadhguru talk about happiness and satisfaction, I wondered how many people were like me. I didn't think of myself as unhappy, but rather dissatisfied or unfulfilled. I thought there might be a lot of people out there like me who really didn't know what we were missing, and Sadhguru was saying that there was definitely something missing.

While Sadhguru was talking, I drifted off into a daydream and suddenly thought about one of the video jobs I did with Jennifer that was on the subject of 401(k) retirement plans. We visited companies and interviewed employees who were currently participating in their savings plan, and we asked them questions about retirement. In all, we talked to over thirty employees—young and old, rich and poor—and we heard the same story over and over.

"When I retire, I'm going to do the things I want to do and have fun with my life," said one middle-aged woman.

"When I retire, I'd like to live on the beach," said a young woman. "I think that would be picture-perfect."

"When I retire, I'd like to open my own small shop," said a young man. "Maybe a restaurant or something where I can be my own boss."

"When I retire," said an older woman, "I'm going to get a bunch of women together where we can sew and make quilts and do whatever we want."

In other words, "Someday, I'll be happy."

Many of my coworkers talked longingly about the number of years until they could take early retirement. These were the same people who were afraid to try anything new and who were the most fearful about losing their jobs.

One of the roundtable attendees, a manager named Reese, had asked Sadhguru a question related to this dilemma. Reese wanted to know the same thing many of us did: how much money does a person really need to be happy and comfortable; or, in other words, how much is enough?

"If you observe yourself," Sadhguru said, "one thing that you will see is whoever you are right now, whatever you are right now, there is something within you which is longing to be a little more than what you are right now. However rich you are, however big you are, however powerful you are, whatever you may be—either you are in the dumps or at the peak. Whichever way, you are longing to be a little more than you are right now."

Sadhguru adjusted his long, flowing shawl so that it covered the right side of his chest and shoulder. He then continued, "The currencies may change from education to money, career to something else. It doesn't matter what currency people use. There is something within you which is longing to be a little more than what you are right now. If you observe this longing carefully, if you really give it a keen observation, you will see this longing is not going to stop anywhere in particular. Even if we make you the king or queen of this planet, will you be fulfilled? No, because next you will look up at the stars."

As I listened to Sadhguru talk about our longing to be more than we are, I thought about the founder of the company where I worked. He started by writing his own newspaper, printing it himself, and selling it on the street corners.

Eventually, he had his own building with a handful of employees, and he stopped writing and selling and stepped back to manage the business. I thought he should have been happy enough with that successful business, but instead he began buying other newspapers across the country, creating a business empire. I thought that might be a good place to stop, but instead this guy decided he could run the entire state, so he ran for governor and won the election.

I thought being governor might have satisfied his need to be a little more than he was, but instead he decided to run for president of the United States. This time, however, his dream ended up in a stunning, lopsided defeat. He went back to running the newspaper that he originally started. Maybe in the end, he learned an important lesson: at some point, enough is enough.

"There is something within you which is longing for unbounded expansion," Sadhguru continued. "And, if you seek infinite expansion through physical means, obviously you will be frustrated. It is like you are riding a horse but you want to go to the moon. Someone tells you, if you really whip that horse, you will get there. Maybe you will kill the horse, but you will not go to the moon. If you need to go to the moon, you need a more appropriate vehicle; otherwise, you won't get there."

"Sometimes I feel like that horse," said Reese. "I don't really know where I'm trying to go, so there's no way I'm going to get there."

Sadhguru looked at Reese and studied him for a moment.

"The daily process of going to work and doing what you have to do," Sadhguru continued, "either you are doing something because you want to create something that you think is worthwhile, or you are doing something just to earn a living. You must first decide what is the purpose of your work? If you are just working to earn a living, then you must decide, how much is enough for you? Because if you look all over the world, there is no end to it. However much you have, there will be somebody which has a little more than you. So it's an endless race. If you just basically want to live comfortably, with some sense of security in the world," Sadhguru explained, "then you must decide how much comfort and security is necessary, and just limit your life to that. Or, if you are creating something that you think is worthwhile for the world, there is no limit on how much work you want to do. Because when you are creating something that you care to do, what is the problem if you get an opportunity to work twenty-four hours of the day?"

"I wish I could find something like that to do," Reese said. "Right now I'm just doing something I have to do to earn a living."

"If you make your life, every moment of your life, an expression of your joy, then whatever the type of work that you end up with is not the issue," Sadhguru explained.

I thought about that exchange and realized that for me, finding fulfilling work was the key to finding happiness in my work-life now, not in some distant 401(k) future.

For many people, it might mean having the courage to reinvent their career, find a new job, or start their own business doing something truly meaningful. The only problem was deciding what to do and having the courage to do it.

4

Life's Calling

Sometimes, as I drove around town, I would look at the large office buildings and see people working in the windows. They were sitting at their desks, looking for something in a drawer, putting some paperwork away, talking on the phone, drawing something on a whiteboard, or having meetings. Never did I see anyone just looking out the window enjoying the beautiful view of the city. In fact, many of the people in these windows seemed to have turned their desks so they didn't have to face the outside. I sometimes wondered what it would be like to work in one of those glass towers and have an office with a window. If I ever did, I would be sure to remember to look out and enjoy the view.

Even though I had worked in the past for many large businesses, I had always been a consultant, never an employee. I would come and go using my contractor badge, attend meetings, and then quickly exit, timing my visits to avoid the morning or afternoon rush hour. Luckily, most of my work was accomplished in my home office, which required a morning commute of ten steps down into the basement. However, all of that soon changed.

About six months before meeting Sadhguru, I found myself working inside one of those towering glass monoliths. My cubical was deep within the belly of the beast, far away from the windows. I didn't know whether it was day or night, raining or sunny. There was just my computer monitor, a keyboard and mouse, some drawers to store files, and a gray, fabric-covered cubical wall. That was my situation for eight hours each day.

One thing that I thought was bizarre about corporate life was the interviewing and hiring process. You didn't just meet with a manager and talk about the job and your qualifications. First, you'd interview with other team members whose job was to act like the membership committee at a fraternity or sorority to decide whether you had the right chemistry for the job. Then, there were a series of personality tests that determined if you had the right mind-set for the job. If you passed, the final step was an appointment with an industrial psychologist, who put you through another series of IQ and personality tests and then conducted a face-to-face interview.

"You can do anything you want to," the psychologist told me in my interview. "Why do you want to work for this company?"

"I've had my own business for twenty years," I answered. "But, I lost a lot of my clients after nine-eleven. It's time to reinvent myself somewhere else."

That's essentially what I was forced to do: reinvent myself. In this new job, I would be writing technical documentation in order to collect the smallest paycheck I'd seen since my early days out of college. But, I felt lucky to have a job. At the same time, I didn't know if I was doing the right thing. Maybe I should have tried harder to rekindle my own business before going to work for someone else.

So, when it was my turn to ask Sadhguru a question during the business roundtable, I asked, "How do I know I'm fulfilling my true life's calling?"

"I know a lot of people are going about always thinking in terms of what is their life's calling," Sadhguru began. "What they are meant to be. That's odd. What they're looking for is some God-ordained direction for their life. These problems come because people are not able to make decisions.

"Now, let's say you are a rock star or an astronaut. Neither of these were possible a hundred years ago, isn't it? Whatever is the most popular thing to do, people make that their life's calling. Right now, people think being a basketball star is their life's calling. Throwing balls into baskets cannot be a life's calling. Because right now the game is available and you seem to be good at it, you go ahead for it. You develop a passion for doing something. Now, always people are thinking in terms of, what's my passion?"

When Sadhguru said the word "passion," I thought back to when I had my own business. I had always felt passionate about my work. I had written and produced educational videos and multimedia programs that had helped thousands of people learn about computers. I had produced my own television series, trained police officers, and even helped train rocket scientists. But now, I had no passion for what I was doing. I was just trading my time in exchange for a paycheck. I had no ownership, no involvement, and no incentive to really care. In some ways, I felt like I was going through a midlife crisis, but luckily, so far, I had stayed clear of Corvettes, motorcycles, and extramarital affairs.

"If you don't have passion for something, you shouldn't be doing it," Sadhguru offered. "There is no way to live this life with any sense of enthusiasm and vibrancy, unless you're passionate about it. There should be nothing in your life that you're not passionate about. If you're passionate about every aspect of your life, then you deeply involve yourself with every aspect of your life. When you're involving yourself with everything that you're exposed to, very easily you will find what you're really good at."

Sadhguru looked up for a moment, paused, and then added, "Your life's calling is your ultimate nature. If you look deep down into who you are, then there's no limit to it. When there's no limit to who you really are, then what you do is just in terms of what's needed right now. Whatever is most needed right now in the society, whatever is most needed in the world today, that should be your calling. Your calling should not be your fancy; your calling should be what's needed right now."

His words resonated as I made another entry in my notebook. I wrote and underlined his statement, "Your calling should not be your fancy; your calling should be what's needed right now." I knew that Sadhguru's words applied to all sorts of situations in the world—and they did not necessarily mean to quit your job and join the Peace Corps. To me it meant that your calling should not be whatever you think is the most fun job. Instead, you should look around at the state of the world or the people around you and figure out what you can do to help. In fact, I realized that is the true meaning of life. You come here, you look around and see what is needed in the world, and you get to work making it better for those who come after you.

➤ 5 ◄

Clarity of Perception

As we continued our Q&A with Sadhguru, I asked a follow-up question: "I've worked so hard for over twenty years, doing what I thought I was meant to do. But now after all those years of effort, it's gone. I don't understand what went wrong. Why did this happen to me?"

Sadhguru looked at me for a moment, closed his eyes to look inward, and then answered, "You need to take a look at yourself. If you have assumed a sense of all-knowingness, then you will miss the whole point."

His words hit me like a punch in the stomach.

"So when success is not happening," Sadhguru continued, "there are many, many people who keep on thinking like this, 'My product is better than his. Why is his selling better?' Your product may be better, but maybe your marketing is not good. Your product may be better, but maybe you are not visible for some reason. There are so many aspects," he said pointedly.

"Business is not just about producing something," Sadhguru said, looking me in the eye. "Business is about conducting the whole affair. Today one person produces, one person distributes, another person markets, and another person advertises. Like this it is being divided, because the same talent and capabilities are not present in everybody. But whatever business you are doing, you must be looking constantly to see what the loophole is. Generally, people are not able to see the loopholes in their life.

"Are you okay for a story?" Sadhguru asked.

I nodded.

"It happened once, there was a parish priest in a small town," Sadhguru recounted. "It happened to be his birthday. So, some of the children who attended his Sunday school brought some gifts. One little boy brought a gift-wrapped box. The moment the priest saw this, he said, 'Jeff, you have brought me a book. Very nice.'

"Jeff said, 'But Father, how did you know?'

"The priest said, 'Oh, Father knows everything.'

Jeff's father happened to own a bookstore. Everybody knows this in the town. Another little girl brought another gift. The priest looked at the gift-wrap and said, 'Oh Mary, you brought me a sweater.'

"And the little girl was totally amazed. 'Father, how did you know?'

"The priest said, 'Oh, Father knows everything.' The little girl's father happens to own a woolen store. And then little Tommy brought another gift. And the Father noticed it was leaking a little bit. And little Tommy's father owns a liquor shop. So the priest said, 'Oh, Tommy, you brought me a bottle of wine.'

"Tommy said, 'No, you are wrong.'

"'Okay, you have brought me a bottle of rum.'

"Tommy said, 'No, not at all, you are wrong.'

"Then the priest put his hand to the leaking gift-wrap, touched it, and put it in his mouth, and asked, 'Is this gin?'

"Little Tommy said, 'No, Father, I brought you a puppy!'"

After we stopped laughing, Sadhguru continued his answer. "You will end up with the wrong taste in your mouth, if you have assumed a sense of all-knowingness. You must read every situation for what it is. And situations are constantly evolving. If you want to be in business, you have to evolve, too. Not just the business situation, but evolving yourself. Any work that you do must be an opportunity for you to grow; otherwise, what's the point? If you do not use every work situation for your own internal growth, if you do not use every situation that you face—challenging or otherwise—to improve yourself, the way you are as a human being, then somewhere you will be left out. Either you will be left out of the money, or you will be left out of happiness, or you will be left out of peace, or left out of success. In one way or the other, life will leave you out."

I had a sudden realization about my own career. I had become stale, doing the same thing the same way for too many years. I had not grown or evolved; I had just been treading water. In my business I had relied on a few long-time customers and had not tried to find new ones and new things to do. I had not challenged myself or looked for ways to improve. Sadhguru seemed to hit the nail on the head regarding my situation.

Sadhguru continued to explain: "You're successful when you have a certain clarity about what needs to happen. It does not come from reading books. You must be able to look at situations and see where the situation would evolve within the next moment or the next day or the next year or the next decade. "This happened to a major newspaper house in India," he recounted. "When this particular person inherited this newspaper business from his father, it was in bad shape. This was one of the minor businesses for him. There were other industries and things which were much bigger in terms of money. But this person closed down all the other businesses and just took up this one newspaper. His family definitely thought that he had gone insane. In the business community, it was a joke that the fool gave up his strength and went for his weakness. But in about fifteen years, this newspaper house became the leading newspaper in the country and one of the largest-selling newspapers in the world, selling over one million copies per day. He did not know much about the newspaper business—he is not a journalist—but he just had a certain clarity about what people want to read, what people would like to read today, what people may want to read ten years later. Just having this clarity, his business just grew. For this man, his clarity came because he started meditating. When he looked at all the businesses and what could happen to them, he was able to think clearly, see things very clearly without being bogged down by the existing situation.

"One who is truly successful is a man who is not influenced by the existing situation," Sadhguru emphasized, "the existing situation of success or failure, the existing situation of poverty or opulence, not being bogged down by that, but just able to see where it's evolving tomorrow.

"So in his mind, he saw of all the businesses that his family owned, it was that newspaper which was going to grow. It was the newspaper which had the unlimited possibilities in the country. And, he went for it against all advice. He went for it against all the so-called business sense. This bold decision came because he was meditating, and he had the clarity to make the decision.

"Only a meditative mind which is not at all enslaved to whatever the past experiences of life are, or whatever the existing situations are, can see what is happening now or what is going to happen tomorrow with clarity," Sadhguru explained. "If you want to be successful with any activity, this clarity is absolutely necessary, and that clarity can be brought forth in every human being.

"We had the opportunity to train the Indian field hockey team. Field hockey is India's national game. We just had only five days to train these boys. They're all highly talented, but there was a phase of a few years where they barely won any international matches. On their home ground they were doing well, but when they went to another country, they would not always produce the results.

"Some simple yogic practices were brought into their lives, which brings a certain sense of ease within you, so that you tend to walk through life effortlessly. Once this came, one particular player who is responsible for scoring goals, over the next three months the number of goals that he scored were phenomenally high for his career. The fundamental thing that we taught him was how to see himself playing field hockey.

"As a child, he started playing hockey because he liked to hit the ball. He enjoys hitting the ball and that's all it's about. That's all hockey is really about. Once you're doing what you really enjoy doing, you will put all of yourself into it. "This is not about winning a match. The other team members must have strategies to get the ball to you, but once the ball comes, you just have to hit the ball in the right direction with the right speed. So, what is needed is just that you enjoy the game totally. He had always enjoyed the game, but he didn't really enjoy playing in an important match because there was so much stress on him to help the entire country win. He has the expectations of one billion people behind him.

"The moment he learned to be at ease with his own body and his mind, forget about the match, forget about the country, all he remembers now is that he wants to hit the ball and suddenly he started scoring so much better.

"It doesn't matter what work you've chosen," Sadhguru said, looking back at me. "You took this work because that's what you want to do in some way. You want to do it for whatever reason. You want to do it for money, or you want to do it for your family, or you want to do it just for the fun of it; it doesn't matter. If you've chosen to do the work, it means that you want to do it for some meaningful reason. Once you know you want to do it, you give yourself to it with total involvement. Once there is total involvement, there is a joy about doing whatever you're doing."

Sadhguru continued, "What I have found is with certain executives, top executives who are running their own businesses, reasonable large businesses which have international operations, their work schedule was going fourteen to sixteen hours a day. They barely had any time to come home, or when they did come home they are too tired. This is how their condition used to be.

"One particular executive, he used to work at least twelve to sixteen hours a day," Sadhguru explained. "After he started meditating, he found that he could cut down his work considerably. He went to work at eight-thirty in the morning, came home at one o'clock, and that's it. His whole afternoon and evening is free. He spends another two hours on the computer at night and that's it. This man used to go to work at eight-thirty in the morning and come back home at nine or ten in the night. Suddenly, he comes back at one o'clock and, over five years, he has multiplied the value of his business by six or seven times, because of his own clarity and his ability to lead people better.

"So once a person is at ease within himself, naturally he functions at his best. Bringing this sense of ease within himself, bringing this sense of effortlessness within you is most essential. Inner Engineering is just this, to engineer your interiority so that you function effortlessly. Effortless living within yourself does not mean you avoid challenging situations. When you are effortless within yourself, you seek challenging situations. You are not avoiding them anymore."

Sadhguru's story reminded me of my previous self-employed life, where for twenty years I set my own hours and worked when I wanted to work. I had been totally involved in every aspect of our business, so much so that it didn't seem like work.

My new job was completely different. I worked regular business hours and was expected to be in my office working during that time, regardless of whether it was productive time. I was not totally involved, and, as a result, I was not happy. I knew I had to find a way to change that; I needed to meditate and use the clarity it brings to pinpoint where and how to become totally involved.

6

Inner Engineering

About a year before the business roundtable talk and before I had met Sadhguru, I had just started my new midlife crisis job and was slowly getting sucked into the nine-to-five routine. I wasn't used to the morning and evening rush-hour traffic that so many people have accepted as a normal part of life—the stop and start, cars darting in and out, horns honking, people tailgating while talking on cell phones, and eating, reading, and applying makeup while driving. When I came home from work, I often had a glass of wine or a beer to shift my mind away from running with the rats on the freeway to something different, such as the evening news with its wonderful assortment of end-of-the-world stories.

To avoid the traffic, I started leaving home at 5:30 a.m., arriving at the office shortly after 6:00. If I left home any time after 6:15, it usually took over an hour to get to the office. In the afternoon, I tried to leave at 4:00 p.m., but this was often too late to avoid the rush, so it always took me at least an hour or more to get home. Sometimes, I would wait until after traffic to come home, leaving the office after 7:00 p.m. These thirteen-hour days were zapping my energy and leaving Jennifer feeling abandoned.

About two months into my new job, Jennifer became depressed about our situation. Over the past year, our friends and family had experienced a series of sicknesses and injuries. One of our best friends, Eric, who had worked with us for years on video productions, and who had introduced us to yoga, had been diagnosed with bone marrow cancer. Jennifer had spent a lot of time taking care of Eric, fixing him meals, taking him to the doctor, and helping with his home-dialysis treatments.

As Eric was dying, we suddenly got a call that my elderly father had fallen and broken his leg. A few days later, my mother fell and hit her head, and the two of them ended up in the same hospital room. Jennifer and I left everything and drove to Texas and spent several weeks taking care of them. While we were there, Eric died, and Jennifer flew back for his wake, while I stayed with my parents.

The entire year had been like this. No sooner had we returned home and settled into our normal routine than we got another call that my mother had fallen and broken her hip. We turned around and went back to Texas and helped with my mother's rehab.

At this point, we talked with my parents about their moving from the small Texas town where they had lived for the past twenty years to be closer to us. After some initial reluctance, they finally agreed, and we began an arduous moving process. Jennifer spent six weeks getting their belongings packed and cleaning out twenty years of clutter. She came back home and found a house for my parents about five minutes away from our place, and then coordinated the moving company, and helped get the old place ready to sell.

By the end of the year, Jennifer was exhausted, and when January came around, she sank into a depression. She stayed in bed or on the sofa in the living room, wore her pajamas all day, and didn't want to eat.

I tried to prod her out of her depression, but she repeatedly told me there was only one thing I could do to help: "Quit your job." We argued about this several times. Jennifer wanted us to try to get our business going again, but I didn't know where we would find new clients. Many of our previous customers had vanished just after 9-11 when the economy had taken a nosedive.

"Besides, I've already got a job," I told her. "And it comes with a pension, a 401(k) plan, and two weeks of vacation. I'm not quitting."

One Sunday, while Jennifer was lying on the couch moping, I was sorting through sections of the newspaper. I grabbed the business and sports sections and tossed the classifieds and other parts of the paper that we didn't read on the floor. The last section to hit the floor was the Faith and Values section. It landed with a plop, and there on the front page was a large picture of Sadhguru. It instantly caught Jennifer's eye.

"Look at that guy," she said as she peered over the picture of the man with the fluffy white beard wearing a turban.

"He looks like Santa Claus," I commented.

Ignoring me, she picked up the paper and began reading the article about a visiting Indian yogi who was teaching "an intensive meditation workshop." She learned that there was an introductory talk the next evening and that a meditation class would be taught starting Wednesday night.

"I have to go do this," she told me. "If Eric were still alive, he'd tell me to go."

"Sure, go ahead!" I responded, happy that she was interested in something, anything.

"Do you want to go with me?" she asked.

"No," I said. "You go check it out."

I ended up working late on Monday night when Jennifer went to the introductory talk. I got home before she did, and she joined me about an hour later. When she arrived, she told me, "This guy is amazing! He's real. There's something about him that I can't describe. Whatever it is, I have to find out more about it."

"Are you going to take the class?" I asked.

"Yes," Jennifer said, "I went ahead and signed up."

"Good. Maybe this will pull you out of your funk."

"Do you want to take the class, too?" she asked. "There's still time to sign up."

"No," I told her. "You see what it's about, then maybe I'll take the next one."

"He's come all the way from India to teach this," Jennifer explained. "There may not be a next one."

"That's okay," I told her, as I was too wrapped up emotionally in my work to really understand the meaning of this opportunity. I added, "You learn it and then you can teach me."

After Jennifer began the class, I asked how it was going.

"It's going fine," she smiled. And that was all she would say. She didn't elaborate on what happened during the class or how the meditation worked.

When she finished the class and started the yoga practice and meditation in our guest room, Jennifer kept the door closed, so I never saw what was involved in her practice.

At one point, my curiosity got to me, and I asked, "Can I watch you do your yoga practice?"

She knew I wanted to see it in order to perhaps learn how to do it myself, so she answered, "Sure, you can watch, but it's not something you learn by imitating me. It has to be imparted to you from the right source. If you're really interested, you'll have to take the next class."

Over the next few months, I noticed some changes in Jennifer. She looked happier and healthier, and she had miraculously bounced out of her depression. I didn't understand how this yoga and meditation worked, but I could see that it was transforming Jennifer's life, so I decided I needed to try it, too.

A few months later, Sadhguru returned to teach the same class Jennifer had taken, so I eagerly went to hear his introductory talk. I took a seat in a folding chair in the middle of the hotel ballroom. A chair had been positioned on a raised platform for Sadhguru that was surrounded by a beautiful arrangement of tropical flowers.

Sadhguru entered the room from a side door, looked out at the audience, and smiled. Several people in the audience stood out of respect as Sadhguru stepped up onto the platform and sat down in the chair.

After sitting with his eyes closed for a few moments, Sadhguru began to sing. It was a melody I had never heard in a language that sounded ancient. As he sang, I could feel the song resonating deep inside me. I shuddered, sensing the significance of this moment, but I was not able to put it into words or thoughts. After singing for what seemed like five minutes or more, Sadhguru opened his eyes and began his discourse.

"The word 'engineering' fundamentally means that we want to change the situation from the way it is to the way we want it," he said in impeccable English. "That's what engineering means. Whether you build a house, or you build a bridge, or you build a power station, or a nuclear reactor, or whatever, all the engineering involved is fundamentally to change the existing situation into the way we want it. So, that's the external engineering.

"When it comes to the internal, how would you want to be?" Sadhguru said, pointing to his chest. "What kind of a person would you want to be? What kind of inner states do you want to have? If you look at this, you will see, to your amazement, everybody in the world wants only one way to be. Everybody wants to be happy. Everybody wants to be joyful and peaceful. If they do not know anything beyond, at least this much they want. Everybody wants to be in the best possible way a human being can be within himself."

As I watched Sadhguru talk, I realized that all of the people I watched inch along on the freeways each day, all of the people I saw working in those glass office tower windows, all of the people who sat around me each day talking techno jargon, all of the people who went home, poured a glass of wine or popped open a beer and learned about the sad state of the world on the evening news, all of them were trying to find happiness. Even the lowest criminal was essentially trying to find happiness, whether it be in a bottle, a pill, a needle, or from the end of a gun. People committed crimes in a twisted attempt to find happiness for themselves. "Where is it?" I thought to myself. "Is happiness really possible?" At that moment, my mind suddenly snapped back to Sadhguru in mid-sentence.

"Right now, he has written himself off, that such a thing is not possible," Sadhguru continued, seemingly reading my thoughts. "Oh, how can I be happy with a boss like this?" Sadhguru asked. "How can I be happy with a wife like this? How can I be happy with a neighbor like this? Like this they have written themselves off. With these kinds of work situations, these are the conclusions they have made.

"So creating what we want within ourselves is inner engineering," Sadhguru explained. "When we try to engineer physical, material, or social situations the way we want them, there are many forces working upon that. But when it comes to the inner situation, you are the only entity. This should be easy to do. But you find that's the most difficult thing to do, simply because never before have you looked at it in the right direction.

"And another thing is that most people have taken this attitude, 'This is the way I am,'" Sadhguru said as he continued this mindreading game. "Whatever limitations you have in your life, you have enshrined them as yourself. You are so desperate to find some identity for yourself. Because of the desperation of wanting to be identified with something, you have gotten yourself identified with certain limitations of function within you. Because of these identifications, you are unwilling to change, because if you change you would lose those identities. The moment you get identified with your limitations, how can you leave them? Suppose you get identified with poverty. Can you ever become rich? Suppose you get identified with hunger. Can you ever eat properly? Suppose you get identified with your ill health. Can you ever become healthy? Similarly, if you get identified with your anger, with your irritation, with your unhappiness, with your depression, you can never be otherwise."

I was suddenly very uncomfortable. He seemed to be hearing my pleas for help, and he was addressing them directly. Could he really read minds? I wondered about the rest of the people in the room. Was Sadhguru just talking to me? Of course not. Most of the people in the room were just as unfulfilled and dissatisfied as I was. Most of us were thinking the same things about our simple lives.

"So the first thing is to see that what you are right now, what kind of human being you are right now is your creation," Sadhguru explained. "And ninety percent of it or more has been created unconsciously. So you created yourself, but unconsciously.

"Now that you have become aware, functioning like this is becoming hazardous for yourself," Sadhguru continued. "To live in this world and to get irritated with little things is hazardous. Because that means you can't go into the world and do whatever you want to do. You have to live in protected atmospheres. If you are going to be disturbed by external situations, that means you have a handicap. If you are going to get angry when things don't go the way you want them to go, that means you have decided to limit your life. You have decided to limit the scope and possibilities of your life the moment you are capable of being irritated or getting angry or sad or depressed.

"So, now you want to engineer yourself the way you want yourself to be. If you look at this, definitely you want yourself to be free from all these things which limit your life. So can you do it? Definitely, because whatever distress that you are going through within yourself, is either of the body, or of the mind, or your energies have become volatile, or your very chemistry is going crazy.

"Let's say you lost your peace today," Sadhguru suggested. "If you lose your peace, what happens? You start yelling at people who live with you in your family. If it continues, maybe tomorrow you will pick a quarrel with your neighbor. If it continues, tomorrow you go to your office and yell at your boss. The moment you yell at your boss, everybody around you knows that you need medical help!"

The audience laughed, and it helped ease the tension that had been building within me.

Sadhguru then continued. "When you yelled at your wife, they thought it's normal. But when you yell at your boss, people know you need medical help. So they take you to your doctor. Initially the doctor tries to talk you out of it, but most of the time it doesn't work. So, he puts a pill into you. A pill means a certain amount of chemicals. This little bit of chemical goes into your system and makes you peaceful. Even if it is just for a short while, you do become peaceful. Or, in other words, what you call as 'peace' is a certain kind of chemistry. What you call as 'joy' is another kind of chemistry. What you call as 'anxiety' is another kind of chemistry. Agony, ecstasy, every human experience has a chemical basis to it. Now, what I am talking about is creating the right kind of chemistry without a pill.

"There is a whole science—an inner science, the yogic science—through which you can create an inner chemistry which is peaceful and joyful by its own nature," Sadhguru explained. "Now you are no more looking for peace and joy in your life. You are peaceful and joyful by your own nature. Now, your life is just an expression of this joy. Now, whatever kind of situations you are placed in, whatever kind of challenges you may have to take up in your life, it is no longer stressful.

"Once you are no longer concerned about whether you will lose your happiness or peace, when this concern is not there, you can take up any challenge in the world," Sadhguru explained. "Things that you have never imagined in your life, you can take it up and do it because there is no more concern about what will happen to me. Because whatever happens to me this is the way I am. This will not change. Once this assurance is there for you, you can even take a contract in hell, and happily do the work. What's your problem? Especially if there is a hell, that's the place where you need to go and air-condition the place because they say it's very hot. You could have a good air-conditioning contract there, isn't it?"

The introductory talk continued for another hour until Sadhguru stopped to answer questions. People wanted to know if inner engineering would improve their health, if it would help them in business, and if it would help save their marriages. Sadhguru patiently answered each one with detailed explanations that described yoga as a technology that could transform your life, if you took it seriously.

The session had ended and, as a group of people gathered around Sadhguru to ask him personal questions, I sat for a few moments and thought about what I'd just heard. Would Sadhguru's yoga help me with my career decisions? Could it help me control my anger and frustration? I knew it had helped Jennifer, so I decided to give it a try. I went to the registration table and signed up for the class.

Sadhguru conducted the class personally with the help of volunteers who prepared the classroom, demonstrated yoga techniques, and prepared snacks and meals. The class consisted of talks by Sadhguru, question and answer sessions, and yoga instruction.

Sadhguru started the class by explaining the meaning of yoga: "When we say 'yoga,' we don't mean impossible pretzel poses. That's not what we're referring to. Yoga means to be in perfect tune. Your body, mind, and energy and the existence are in absolute harmony."

Later that first evening, Sadhguru talked about yoga's effect on your body's energy.

"What you call as 'myself' is just a certain amount of energy," Sadhguru explained. "Do you know, modern science is telling you that the whole existence is just energy manifesting itself in different ways? If so, then you're also just a little bit of energy functioning in a particular way. As far as science is concerned, this same energy which you call as myself, can be here as a rock, lie there as mud, stand up as a tree, bark like a dog, or sit here as you. Everything is the same energy, but functioning at different levels of capability.

"Similarly, among human beings, though we're all made of the same energy, we still don't function at the same level of capability. What you call capability or talent, what you call your ability to do things in the world, your creativity, is just a certain way your energy functions. If you gain a little bit of mastery over your own energies, you will do things that you never imagined possible."

Later, Sadhguru turned the discussion toward awareness. He explained it like this: "If you are sitting here as a bundle of thoughts, opinions, and emotions, you will never know what's needed. Most people are like this. What you call a human being is really not a being; it is just a bundle of thoughts, emotions, and opinions that were gathered from elsewhere."

How true, I thought. Many of us have opinions, but those opinions are formed from what we hear on the TV or radio or read in the newspaper. None of us really knows the truth, unless you witness a situation firsthand. Then, depending on what you see, your emotions and past experiences paint your descriptions according to your own point of view. This was true about life and true about business.

"If you can simply sit here as *life*," Sadhguru continued, "you always know. You will always know what's needed. You don't need to think about it. You don't have to educate yourself to know. Any human being who is able to sit here as *life* will simply know what the other beings around him need."

I wondered what he meant by "sitting here as life." I assumed it was a state of openness that came from doing meditation. I would later learn this to be true. After I had been meditating for some time, I realized it meant to sit without judging or labeling things. To just see things simply for what they are and to know what is needed in any situation. What a great ability this would be in business, to simply sit as life and know what your coworkers and customers needed. I had already sat through numerous corporate training sessions that were all attempting to teach me complicated techniques for doing the same thing. In reality, none of them really worked, unless you practiced them to the point that your business life became robotic. And who really wanted to do business with a robot?

"You must cultivate awareness in the most difficult of circumstances," Sadhguru explained. "If somebody abuses you, to abuse him back doesn't require any awareness. But, to remain quiet, you need enormous awareness."

I would later learn from experience that the way you respond in difficult situations is key to your inner growth and strength of character, especially in business situations. When other people are pointing fingers and blaming someone else for the problem, if you remain calm and deal with the situation, it rubs off on the people around you, and they calm down and try to help rather than argue, make excuses, or blame.

Interposed through these interesting discussions was a lesson in simple yoga and meditation, demonstrated by Sadhguru, that took less than thirty minutes a day to complete. I found the practice to be very relaxing and calming.

When the class was over, I was sorry to see it come to an end. I enjoyed spending time with Sadhguru and being moved by his incredible insights into the nature of life. The last few days, we refined our yoga practice with the help of volunteers so that we would be able to do it on our own without any further assistance.

Since I was getting to work by 6:00 a.m., I did my new yoga practice in the gym or in my office. I did my meditation sometimes sitting outside in a small park next to our office building. As I sat, I could sometimes feel a connection with the trees. Each breath I took, the trees had previously exhaled. Each time I exhaled, I gave something back to the trees to inhale. The trees were truly a part of me, as without them I could not exist on this earth.

If my mind was wrapped up in business issues, when I took time for my meditation, I found a completely new perspective on the situation. Fresh ideas and exciting possibilities suddenly danced in my head, where fear and anxiety used to stand like fences. Before taking the class, I had been filled with anxiety about my job and the future. Within just a few weeks, all of that was gone.

I began to notice changes in my awareness and the way I handled situations. I was nicer to people. I made an effort to say hello to people I passed in the halls, and I was more aware of what my coworkers needed, as employees and as human beings.

Probably one of the most noticeable changes was the way I handled rush-hour traffic. I was no longer interested in enforcing my rights as a motorist.

When I saw someone who wanted to cut in front of me, I no longer sped up to try and block them. Instead, I slowed down and made a space. I was no longer angered by the long commute and used the time to improve myself by listening to audio college courses on subjects like psychology, physics, and history. I had gone from road rage to road sage, all by investing a half hour each day to take care of my own inner engineering.

The Human Side of Human Resources

At the time of the business roundtable with Sadhguru, I had been working in a human resources department at a Fortune 500 company for about a year. As I got to know my coworkers and the office politics that swirled through the halls and conference rooms, several things struck me as odd. For one, the people didn't socialize much, or at least they didn't with me. A few people ate lunch together in small groups in the company cafeteria; however, most took food back to their offices and ate lunch alone at their desks.

I noticed a lot of behind-the-back gossiping about the work ethic of various departments. Each department was like a clan that hunted and camped together and didn't trust the other clans that lived nearby on the other side of the glass tower. HR had a love-hate relationship with IT. The two departments had to collaborate on various projects, and each one blamed the other for any problems that occurred.

Many people had stagnated by doing the same job for ten years or more. Instead of any enthusiasm about their work, they drudged away in a bureaucratic daze. They had long ago given up hope of finding anything better to do, and had attached themselves to a ball and chain called the company pension. This was one of the few companies that still promised a pension, and while it was a wonderful benefit to offer employees, it did cause many people to put their careers on autopilot, as they sat in their chairs and waited for their lives to float by.

I talked to one of my coworkers, Martha, about this. She had worked for the company for almost twenty-five years, the same length of time as our vice president, Samantha. While Samantha had risen up through the company, Martha lagged behind several rungs lower on the organization ladder, stuck for years in the same job.

"Once you get to corporate," Martha explained, "you get put in a box with a label on it. They think this is what you do, and it's the only thing you can do. So, you're stuck. There's nowhere else to go, and nothing you can do. Believe me, I've tried."

Related to Martha's situation was a question Jennifer asked Sadhguru during the business roundtable. Jennifer had managed several large multiyear projects, including working as a production manager on a feature film. She later told me that she wondered about her decision to hire crew people based on their experience. She always hired people based on what they had done in the past, not what they hoped to do one day. With this in mind, Jennifer asked, "When you have to decide who is going to work for you, how do you decide between your idea of what they are right now compared to what they might become?"

Sadhguru closed his eyes for a moment and then looked Jennifer straight in the eye. "If you're handling a large number of people, this is always bound to be there," Sadhguru began. "Different people are reliable and dependable in different types of situations. If you don't have this discernment or judgment about it, then you'll put the wrong people in the wrong place and obviously things don't happen."

"But with some people, their capabilities are already apparent," Jennifer interjected. "Others might have potential, but how can you tell?"

"So, everybody definitely has to be approached in different ways, and that's a judgment that you have to make," said Sadhguru. "If that judgment is not made, you will operate out of the handbook, which may work to some extent, but you will not get the best out of people. Nor will you get the best out of yourself."

Sadhguru motioned in the air with his hands, as if assembling some invisible machine. "If you don't know how to put the different parts of a machine together, then it doesn't function properly.

"So a business is just like that," Sadhguru continued. "People are the ingredients which are going into it. Unless you put them in the right place at the right time, the best results won't come. Somehow managing to get by is not the issue. You want to function at the best possible way; that's the issue. So some sense of discernment and judgment is essential in every given situation when you're handling people and material, isn't it? Both for the material and the people, this discernment and judgment is needed."

"Sometimes it's difficult to judge people like that," Jennifer insisted. "Your decisions as a manager could affect their futures and their lives."

"So this judgment need not be a crippling judgment about someone's capability," Sadhguru responded. "This judgment can be situation-specific. It's always good if the business allows enough room to change things up from time to time. We do this at the ashram. Somebody's very good at doing something. Somebody's very good at doing something else. But once in a while, for short periods of time, we interchange the roles here and there. This one thing may create a little chaos in the existing situation, but it keeps people from becoming uptight in their positions. When they become uptight, any change you want to make, they will sabotage it. So, loosening of the people, in whatever way it's possible, is important. When they are a little loose, they're willing to look at things.

"Somebody has been doing this work for a lifetime," Sadhguru continued. "It does not mean he must end up doing it for the rest of his life. He may do something else better than what he's been doing until now. So just a little bit of loosening the atmosphere in the corporate sector, if it is brought about, it'll be good. But right now people are working with such a sense of insecurity, if you try to pull them from that position to another, they are going to get totally worked up. So, that whole atmosphere has to change. The whole work situation atmosphere has to change.

"That change must be brought about by people at the top," Sadhguru explained. "People at the bottom cannot bring about that change. From the top there needs to be a certain sense of ease, togetherness, and trust where people can say what they want to each other. People can go and say what they want to say, or express themselves, or they can ask for a change of work if they have to, without feeling insecure.

"Somebody may be doing an engineering job, but he may have a feeling that he can do an artist's job better," Sadhguru continued. "But he doesn't dare ask. Suppose I attempt it and it doesn't go well? Maybe I will lose my job. So, give him enough freedom where he can express himself."

Sadhguru painted an imaginary picture in the air with his hand. "Tomorrow at lunch hour, you give him one extra hour and let him try out his artistry. What a mess he's going to be or what a genius he's going to be, you try it out and see," said Sadhguru. "This may affect the existing situation a little bit, but this creates many possibilities, because you don't know what a human being carries within himself.

"Someone who did not have any qualifications and was cleaning the floor can make a wonderful engineer, you don't know," Sadhguru reiterated. "Just give him the possibility. Create programs and schedules where the employees can do these things. Situations like this can be set up. Maybe you can have a whole department that does this type of experimenting.

"Right now, HR departments are there, but they're always seeing how to fix people into their places. Instead of that, HR departments should be looking at how to evolve people's capabilities. They can start by looking at how to try out various roles within the organization."

Working in an HR department myself, I realized how badly our company was missing the boat. With all the psychological testing and the evaluation of working styles, people were hired according to the handbook rather than by their capabilities for future growth. There was no opportunity to experiment with new roles and responsibilities. And for a business that claimed its employees were its greatest asset, it was as if the company was tucking its assets under a mattress rather than investing for the future.

Sadhguru paused for a moment, took a sip of water, and then continued. "So, if certain periods are taken off from work, and these kinds of things are done where people are loosened, then one day, somebody who is doing a very simple job in the company is given a chance to play the role of a CEO, at least in a mock way. He gets to see how it feels. He gets to see how hard it is. He will understand and will respect the position even more. And the way he cooperates in the future will be of a completely different nature."

Sadhguru continued, "If you're not able to get people's involvement, then everything is difficult. Because most people who are doing various jobs in many different rungs in the corporation don't have a clear picture of where the whole business is going. They only know what they're doing. So each individual is doing his own work and after some time, gradually they may start working in ways which are contradictory to each other. It is happening everywhere in governments and corporations. Two different departments are working against each other. This may not even be intentional most of the time, because they have no understanding of where the whole business needs to go."

As I mentioned earlier, this very thing was happening to the business where I worked. The HR and IT departments were working against each other. It was a combination of competing goals and the competing personalities of the managers. Neither HR nor IT had any involvement with actually making money for the business. They were too caught up in their own self-importance to realize that they had become liabilities instead of assets.

"So loosening up the situation," Sadhguru said, nodding his head, "changing of roles at least in a mock way, could do a lot of things. A certain amount of time has to be invested fundamentally in human wellbeing—the individual's wellbeing. Whatever the number of working hours, if a certain amount of time, let's say two to five percent of the time, is dedicated to something for that human being's wellbeing—maybe play a game, maybe meditate—just give them a certain time where it is for their wellbeing."

Sadhguru motioned to the business roundtable audience to include everyone in what he was about to say next. "We must understand that this culture does not happen overnight," he explained. "Culture means it's something that you have to work at. Constantly and slowly it evolves. It will not happen by signing a paper. It will not happen just by adopting a policy. It will happen over a period of time, slowly. If a culture of peacefulness, joyfulness, and togetherness is brought forth in the workplace, definitely the productivity of the place can be greatly enhanced."

Sadhguru turned and looked back at Jennifer, who was looking back at Sadhguru through the viewfinder on her video camera.

"At the end of the workday, people should not be wrecked," Sadhguru continued. "People should not be ruined by work. People are made by work. You go to work because you want to make your life, not ruin your life, isn't it? If that goal is being fulfilled, definitely a person will work with more enthusiasm. Right now the process of working is ruining him, so he is going there only for his financial survival. That's going to be a difficult man to work with."

I thought about how miserable many of my coworkers seemed to be. I have to admit, by the end of most days, I, too, was wrecked. And as I drove home each day, I rarely saw any happy faces among the other commuters. Everyone was working for financial survival, and, in the process, people were being ruined by their work.

"You look at yourself and think: What kind of people would you like to work with?" Sadhguru asked. "Happy people or miserable people? If you look at this, definitely you want to work with happy people because happy people are always flexible and easy to work with. Unhappy people are very rigid and very difficult to work with. And when you're working with people, this is one thing that you must constantly remember; everybody else is expecting the same thing from you. You must do your work joyfully, no matter what it is. When you create this culture over a period of time, you will see working in that place becomes easy, and everybody's potential will find better expression."

Sadhguru's answer to Jennifer's question and the advice he offered inspired me. I thought about what I could do to apply his recommendations for loosening people and allowing their human potential to shine. That was the seed that would eventually grow into a very successful program in our human resources department—a program that we would simply call "Project Bloom."

8

It's Just Business

To complete my indoctrination into corporate political correctness, I enrolled in a company-required diversity training course. Going into the class, I expected it to be about how to treat women and minorities. Instead, I was surprised to learn that the course was about soliciting ideas from people with diverse social and cultural backgrounds. In order for a company to appeal to a diverse array of customers, it needed to solicit input from similar types of employees. With over seventy-five thousand employees, our company had a wealth of untapped ideas.

In the class, I also learned there are many different working and problem-solving styles. There are the quick-actors, the slow-planners, and the wait-and-seers. You needed a good mixture of these types of people on your team in order to have a healthy, productive work group. Essentially, the message was to respect one another and try to play nice.

At first, I wondered if they really needed any more ideas from middle-aged white guys like me. I imagined that was one category where the answer might be, "No, we've had quite enough of that; we're looking for something fresh." How about exploring the impact of meditation on business? Is that fresh enough? At the time, this was the furthest thing from my mind; however, as I look back now at these events, I can see that it was the perfect setup.

Because morale at the company wasn't very good, and there was distrust between departments, the HR department decided to follow the ideas they taught in the diversity class and ask for employee input. They asked everyone to fill out an online survey. The survey asked us to use a scale of "Not at all, Little,

Some, Great, or Very great" to rate the performance of the management team. They asked questions like, "Is management accessible to provide support as necessary? Does management value the contributions of all individuals? Does management create environments that make work enjoyable? Does management show interest in each individual's career? Does management coach others in skill and knowledge development? Does management demonstrate that they can be trusted?"

Later, I would learn that from the survey results, one-third and sometimes half of the responses rated these questions with "Not at all, Little, or Some." Almost half the staff didn't trust their managers and were afraid to say what was really on their minds. And almost half the employees didn't think that management had any interest in their career goals or development.

Needless to say, we were a rather sick organization. While we worked in beautiful offices with nice furniture and state-of-the-art equipment, we were missing the human side of human resources.

We were the true definition of a bureaucracy. The seventy-five thousand employees were treated as numbers and paperwork. We processed health care benefits, pension payments, workplace savings accounts, and disability payments. We didn't have time to consider the human beings whose wellbeing was being approved or denied.

As a result of the employee survey, management decided to solicit employee ideas through a series of forums. Approximately ten employees were invited to each forum to share ideas for making improvements in the department. It was only a month after the business roundtable discussion with Sadhguru, and I was full of ideas inspired by his advice. A couple of days before going to the forum, I put together a proposal for a new kind of diversity team.

I shared the proposal with my wife Jennifer to see what she thought. I remember telling her, "I'm going to be part of a diversity team at work."

She looked at me and giggled. "What did you do wrong?"

"Nothing," I smiled. "It's a chance to apply some of Sadhguru's ideas to business. I'm proposing that we create a diversity team to do some experiments."

I went over the details with Jennifer. The goals were to handle conflict resolution, create more opportunities for social interaction, solicit ideas, develop employee potential, and build something we could share with the rest of the company. We would look for solutions and make recommendations to management.

Not having worked for a large corporation before, I didn't really know how diversity councils operated. I did some research on the Internet and discovered that many companies had them. Many of the councils served to promote the interests of minorities and women in business like I had originally thought before I attended the diversity training. Others were more like advisory boards that served as the voice of the employees to management, almost like an employee union. In some cases, someone from the diversity council sat as part of the board of directors.

After sharing my ideas with Jennifer, she said I should package it together with a theme. "It reminds me of our garden," she said. "A garden has many different plants with different needs. Some need sun; some need shade. Some make nice bushes, some offer beautiful flowers. There are even a few weeds mixed in. It's the same thing with the people in a business. They have different needs and make different contributions. And like plants, they all have the same goal, to flourish and bloom."

After thinking about it for a moment, Jennifer suggested, "Why don't you call it, 'Project Bloom'?"

"That's good," I responded. "I like that."

I finished a short, one-page proposal and took it with me to the forum. One of the HR managers, Rose, hosted the forum and went around the room asking for ideas about ways to make improvements. My coworkers didn't offer much. They complained about the fact that there was little opportunity for advancement. They thought managers were just out for themselves and didn't care about their direct reports. The meeting went on for an hour or more, as we listened to a litany of complaints. Rose took notes and each time asked for ideas on how to remedy the situation. I was amazed that most of the people in my group didn't offer any solutions. They had given up hope and just wanted a chance to vent their frustration. It didn't seem like the right atmosphere to discuss my proposal for Project Bloom, so I left my copy in my briefcase under my chair.

When the meeting was over, I lagged behind and waited for the other employees to leave. Rose was still working on some notes, so I pulled out the proposal and gave it to her.

"This is a proposal for a diversity council called Project Bloom," I told her.

"That sounds interesting," Rose said, looking up from her notes and taking the proposal from me.

"That meeting was too much of a gripe session to talk about it then," I told her.

"I know what you mean," said Rose as she quickly looked over the one-page proposal and smiled. "I'll pass it along with the rest of my notes."

"Thanks," I said and then started for the door.

"Listen," Rose told me with a sympathetic tone. "It's a really good idea; however, they've tried a diversity council here before, and it didn't work. So, don't take it personally if nothing happens; it's just business you know."

I left the room feeling somewhat stunned; all the hope had leaked out of my balloon. I went back to my cubical and wished I had a door I could close. I sat for a few moments and then thought about a question Allan had asked Sadhguru during the business roundtable.

Allan was a real estate broker who often had to deal with competition from other agents who stole his clients. He had asked, "Sometimes in business situations, people say, 'Don't take it personally. It's just business.' How should I respond to statements like this?"

Sadhguru paused for a moment, looked at Allan and, with a slightly tilted head, answered, "If one forgets that whatever we are doing—whether we are doing business or politics or whatever—all this is being done fundamentally for human wellbeing. All the commerce in the world is happening fundamentally for human wellbeing. At least, that's the intention we started with."

"That's interesting," said Allan. "I've never thought about it that way."

"So, if we think it's all right that in the process of doing business we can break people up, there is really no sense to it," Sadhguru explained. "Because every kind of business that we do in the world is only in pursuit of human wellbeing. If wellbeing is not happening to people, then there is no sense to business. And when you work together, when ten people or a hundred people or a thousand people work together, if they do not learn to be concerned about each other's wellbeing, then ultimately the whole business ethos will become such that the business that you are doing will not be of any wellbeing to the world. Anything that's not of any wellbeing to the world will not sell forever. It may sell today, but not tomorrow."

I thought about my own career and the companies that had been my clients over the years. There were several where wellbeing was not their focus. Their focus was on selling and not on the customer or the wellbeing of their employees. As an example, I remember that we were asked to do some video training for a multilevel marketing company. After we researched the company to write the videos, I couldn't see where the company provided any value. It was a pyramid scheme where people at the top got rich by feeding on people from the bottom. After we delivered our training programs to them, they didn't pay the bill. I wasn't surprised to discover that they closed shop a few months later. The sharks at the top had eaten their fill and swam on to another multilevel marketing opportunity in another ocean.

I thought this principle of wellbeing should also be applied when considering employment by a company or when investing in a company's stock. Before taking a new position or buying a share, research the business carefully to make sure that you can identify what the business does to foster human wellbeing. If the business does not support human wellbeing in some obvious way, it won't contribute any long-term value to the world. So, why waste your life as an employee or your money as an investor with an organization like that?

Sadhguru continued, "So, if you are in a situation where people do just what they have to do to get by, where they will not reach out and do the extra things that need to be done, if everybody works like this, working in such a place is going to be extremely difficult. And it will be a life-taking experience."

I thought again about what Sadhguru had just said. "If people do just what they have to do to get by, it will be a dull, meaningless workplace." That is exactly what was happening at my company. The employees were doing just what they were told and nothing else.

"Once you have chosen a certain line of work, you spend a large part of your time and life there," Sadhguru continued. "If you don't create a conducive atmosphere for human beings to blossom forth, if human beings cannot be happy and joyful, their intelligence, their body, nothing will work well.

"Today, most of the business atmospheres have become like this, that just in the process of working, people are becoming so sick," Sadhguru said. "So, whatever the success that you seek is actually a curse upon you. Lots of successful people in the world are not happy. Success should have brought you wellbeing. But if it has not brought you wellbeing, then what is the point pursuing it? This is happening because of this attitude that you need not be concerned about anything other than business. Business is people, your fundamental business is people. It's human wellbeing which is the basis of all the businesses in the world. If that is forgotten, then that business is of no relevance to human beings."

I thought about the proposal for Project Bloom being passed around the management meetings. I believed it would transform our business if given the chance. It followed Sadhguru's advice and would change the focus of our organization to human wellbeing. It would result in employees doing that little something extra to show they cared about each other. It could transform morale and fix most of the problems that were uncovered by our employee survey. Project Bloom could do a lot if only management would give it a try. But as Rose had said, my proposal might end up in a compost pile, since they had tried a diversity team in the past and it had failed. This time, something told me it was different. It was time to rewrite the old mantra, "It's only business," and introduce the new one that Sadhguru had suggested: "Business is about human wellbeing."

Leadership by Example

What I respected about my manager, Mike, was that even though he worked from a wheelchair, he didn't use it as an excuse. I learned that he had been injured in a car accident when he was a teenager. A friend had just obtained his driver's license and taken Mike and another friend out for a joyride. The friend had lost control of the car and Mike had been thrown through the back window of the car, resulting in a catastrophic spinal injury.

Mike's story was very similar to my own teenage experience with a friend named Joel. Joel had just obtained his license and came to pick me up for a drive. We had only been driving for a few minutes when Joel began to yell and show off as he drove down a winding neighborhood street. We turned a corner in front of a house where a man was watering his yard and splashed through the water that was running out into the street. The car hydroplaned, Joel overcorrected the steering, and we smashed head-on into a telephone pole. The car was totaled, but both Joel and I walked away.

As I watched Mike working, wheeling his chair into and out of elevators, in and out of meeting rooms, I couldn't help but wonder, what if that had been me?

I told Mike about the Project Bloom proposal, and he listened patiently as I described how it would work. After a few moments, I noticed he was smiling.

"Are you going to have us arranging flowers?" he asked, chuckling.

"I think flowers would be nice," I told him sarcastically.

Mike wasn't far enough up the management food chain to be involved in the recent survey or the forums, so he couldn't tell me how the proposal might have been received.

While Mike did manage three people, primarily he was a project manager, and one of the most well-liked and respected. He could joke when it was appropriate and be serious when that was needed. He could handle negotiations with vendors involving millions of dollars with ease. Mike was a natural-born leader.

I remembered that during the business roundtable discussion with Sadhguru, we had talked about management and leadership. Robert was an executive who had about fifty people who reported to him. He asked Sadhguru, "What does it mean to be a good leader?"

Sadhguru looked at Robert closely, studying him for a moment and then answered, "One aspect of leadership is the people around you should have confidence in you. Confidence comes because they themselves are not able to make decisions, but you're willing to make those decisions. When you make decisions, you're taking the risk of being held responsible for whatever may happen. That is a privilege and that is also the burden of leading a team of people. If you make a wrong decision or a right decision, both ways, the responsibility is always there."

"What if you make the wrong decision?" Robert asked. "Then everyone blames you and your team loses confidence. I'm almost afraid to make a decision without consulting my team."

"So right through the whole process of working together," Sadhguru responded, "if you involve everybody, they need not know that they are making the decision. If you listen to everybody carefully, and get their perception of the whole thing, and then make the decision, then whatever the results are, if you make all of them responsible for the decision, you must share the success with them. Then when something goes wrong, naturally they share that with you, too. And they know a bad decision has been made. We have to correct it, and that's all there is."

"The problem where I work is that I'm the one who is measured by these decisions," Robert explained. "Since I'm the manager, I'm forced to take the credit or the blame."

Sadhguru countered, "But when good things are happening, if you take all the credit, when the bad things happen, naturally they want to point fingers at you and it becomes an ugly situation, and the team will break up, and the future effectiveness of the whole team will be gone."

Sadhguru paused for a moment to let his message sink in and then continued, "So creating a sense of responsibility, creating a sense of involvement in everybody, in everything that's happening, whether it's good, bad, or ugly, it doesn't matter. Whichever way it's going, involving everybody in the process will give you a certain amount of space, so that when things go wrong, you have the necessary space to correct it. Otherwise, when things go wrong, people blame each other and things fall apart."

Robert then interjected, "You were a businessman before you become involved in all this. How did you go about building your business?" I could tell Robert was fishing around to find out if Sadhguru practiced what he preached.

Sadhguru looked at Robert and frowned. "What do you mean I *was* a businessman before? Even now I am a businessman!" Sadhguru laughed heartily, and his whole body shook up and down.

"It's just the goals and the orientation of the business has changed, that's all," Sadhguru continued. "At that time, I was in business to make money. Now, I am doing business to bring wellbeing. At that time, I was in the construction industry. I was building homes and various other types of buildings for people. That was also human wellbeing. But I did not know that. I thought I was building the houses for money. But now I know that after all, everything that you do is for human wellbeing, so now I am just addressing it directly. That's all the difference."

"What about the way you conducted business back then?" Robert asked pointedly. "Did you have to fire people?"

"It's not different!" Sadhguru insisted. "At that time, I had a few hundred employees with me. Today, I have a quarter million volunteers with me. As I managed the business, I have to manage these volunteers; otherwise, this won't work. It's much harder to manage volunteers than employees because at that time, if they didn't work well I could fire them. Now I am working with volunteers, I can't fire them no matter what they do." Sadhguru laughed and was joined by the rest of the room.

"So, I'm not out of business," Sadhguru insisted. "I'm very much into it, more than ever—addressing the fundamental issue of life. Whatever we do, whether you sell coffee, or you build a home, or you manufacture a spacecraft, you are still working toward human wellbeing. But unfortunately, most people have forgotten this. So, whether I teach yoga or I build homes, still I am working for human wellbeing. But now we are just addressing it directly."

"But most people work to make money," Robert interrupted. "They really don't think about human wellbeing. It's all about what's in it for me."

Sadhguru looked at Robert and smiled. "Once the issue of what I am going to get out of it is over, then your business is always successful, because whatever you do anyway brings some wellbeing," he explained. "It's just that you are not aware of it, that's all. As long as you're continuously aware that by doing whatever you are doing, you are making a huge contribution to people's lives, then every activity that you do is successful. It doesn't matter what you do."

"It doesn't?" Robert asked with disbelief.

"If you sit here and just breathe, if you inhale oxygen and exhale carbon dioxide, you're doing a great service to the world," Sadhguru explained. "If you are aware of this, you know how sweet it will be just to sit here and breathe."

"I don't know," Robert complained. "I think most people work for their own personal wellbeing, not everybody else's."

"It is just that people's idea of human wellbeing may be different in terms of proportion," Sadhguru explained. "For one person, human wellbeing may mean just his wellbeing. For another person, human wellbeing may mean him and his family. For another person, it may be his community, or his nation, or the whole world. So it is just a question of proportions. But there is nobody in the world who is not concerned about human wellbeing. Every human being is concerned about human wellbeing. Only in proportion it varies."

"Everyone?" Robert questioned. "What about criminals and other bad people?"

"You know, we are doing a lot of work in the prisons," Sadhguru explained patiently. "About twenty percent of our time, energies, and resources are spent in the prisons, both in India and the outside. So people keep asking me all the time, we are here waiting for you, but you are spending so much time in the prison with those criminals—with murderers, with drug addicts, with rapists, with all kinds of people. Why? As far as I'm concerned, the man whom you call as a criminal is just one more human being who is in pursuit of his happiness. It is just that he is pursuing his happiness far more vigorously than you. So vigorously that he is not concerned about what's happening around him. So in a business environment, maybe there is not yet a law to put you behind bars, but the moment you start functioning in the world, not being concerned about what's happening to life around you, you are a criminal, too."

"Are you saying it is criminal to be a leader who is only out for himself?" Robert asked.

"Whatever the nature of activity we have chosen for our life, if we wish to be leaders in those situations, first thing is we must be able to lead by example,"

Sadhguru explained. "Not by words, not by trickery, not by cunning, but by example."

"So, get your own house in order first?" Robert asked.

"Fundamentally," Sadhguru responded, "your ability to lead people means your ability to take people in a particular direction to achieve a particular goal. If this has to happen, you must be able to inspire them to go on by themselves in that direction. If you have to constantly keep them in line, to get a job done, then it's going to be hugely difficult to be a leader."

"What do you do in those situations?" Robert asked. "My team is spread out across the country. It's very difficult to keep everyone on the same page."

"As the team grows, or if the kind of team that you're managing is beyond physical contact, then leading people in huge numbers is going to be very difficult if you cannot lead them by inspiration," Sadhguru explained. "If you have to inspire people to do whatever is required out of them, you must be that kind of an example. The very way you exist can be that kind of an example, so that people naturally stand up and want to do things that are necessary to be done. You cannot lead people when you have to constantly supervise them and manage them. You can lead people only when people are inspired to do what you want them to do. They get so inspired that they are going to do more than you ever even thought of doing. Only then, leadership becomes an effortless process. So a good leader is able to set a good example; that his way of being, his way of existence itself, is an inspiration for everybody to move in that direction."

It was this answer that made me think about my manager, Mike. Whether he knew it or not, the way he worked from his wheelchair was an inspiration to his team. After a while, you didn't see the wheelchair, but it was in the back of your mind as you watched him working as late as anyone and jumping in to help when it was needed. Mike used his handicap to his advantage as a leader because his teams were always inspired to do even more than what he asked. Mike was already leading by example, but I wondered how much more effective he might be if he also meditated regularly.

Sadhguru stopped and suddenly turned directly to me and asked, "You have a question?"

There was silence in the room, but after a few moments, I realized he was looking straight at me.

"You have a question," Sadhguru insisted.

"Yes," I said surprised. "I was just wondering how meditation could benefit a manager."

"Meditation is not an act," Sadhguru explained. "It's not something that you do; it's something that you become. It's a certain quality. If you cultivate your body, your mind, your emotion, and your energy to a certain level of maturity, meditation will happen. A certain state of being is referred to as meditation. One way of describing this in terms of work would be when you are meditative, you are functioning out of your intelligence, responding to every situation that you face. When you are meditative, the reaction aspect of you is taken off. There is no reaction in you. No matter what kind of situation you're placed in, you are not reactive to it. You are only responding to it. I think for people who lead other people, this is the most invaluable quality in them, that they don't react to situations. They look at everything and respond the way their intelligence and resources allow them to respond in a given situation. Meditation would be truly invaluable for people who want to manage large groups of people."

Sadhguru continued, "Meditation, or being meditative, on another level, means you can play with life whichever way you want, without life really leaving a scratch upon you. Right now, in the process of managing large situations, people are getting wounded, people are getting broken, because instead of managing life, life is managing them, or life is managing to destroy them. Meditation—if meditation comes into the workplace—if people are meditative, even to some extent, their work spaces will become very different. Work spaces would become in such a way that it would be a place that you always love to be. It would be most nurturing for your wellbeing and your health, physically, mentally, in every way. It would be most nurturing for every human being if we create a meditative atmosphere."

"How do you do that in business?" I asked. "Everyone is so busy all the time."

"Creating a meditative atmosphere does not mean that you have to change something about the work," Sadhguru explained. "It is an internal change that you bring about within yourself, that you become a very conscious response to everything, no more an unconscious reaction. The employees will also experience the benefit of this, even if just a few people in the group are truly meditative. Especially those people who are in the key areas of management, if a certain amount of meditativeness is brought into their lives, their effectiveness as managers could be hugely enhanced. It would definitely also bring physical health and mental balance."

Regarding the subject of meditation at work, I was sitting quietly in my cubical one morning before lunch with my eyes closed, doing my meditation. When I slowly opened my eyes, I turned around to find Mike waiting patiently for me a few feet away in his wheelchair.

"Taking a little power nap?" he asked.

"Something like that," I answered.

"Follow me," he said. "There's something I want to show you."

Mike led me out into the hall near the elevators and then turned the corner. He then wheeled his chair into the first open office on the left. I followed him inside and noticed that the office was completely vacant. Mike looked out the large window that overlooked the park, the building's gardens, and the outside dining area below. The gardens had a pond with a curved walkway through the middle that formed a yin-yang symbol when viewed from eleven stories above.

"We did some office shuffling with Benefits, and this office has opened up," Mike explained. "This one is yours now."

I was shocked. My mind instantly flashed to a time years in the past when I had driven past office buildings and looked at the people working inside those glass towers. I was now one of those people with my own private office with a window.

I thanked Mike, and within a couple of hours I had moved in and was working on my computer. As I typed, I heard a low-bass rumble of thunder.

I turned around in my chair and looked out the window to see an enormous thunderstorm approaching from the west. The dark, rolling wall cloud was so low it looked like it would hit the top of our building.

Lightning flashed to the ground across the street in the parking lot of a hotel. As the clouds passed overhead, the trees began to sway violently in the wind, and the building creaked like an old sailing ship. Rain splattered against the window glass, flying through the air sideways and making a clattering sound as it hit the building. I put my feet up on the credenza, leaned back in my chair, put my hands behind my head, and watched nature's spectacle.

I heard someone walk past my office door complaining, "This is really going to mess up the traffic tonight."

I didn't care. I looked out at all the office buildings that seemed to stretch from one end of the horizon to the other. Their architectures of glass reflected the clouds and the storm back from many different angles like fun-house mirrors.

10

The Meditating Manager

After meeting Robert at the business roundtable and listening to his interactions with Sadhguru about leadership, I asked him some questions as he was leaving.

"Do you meditate?" I asked.

"No," Robert said, "but I think I need to learn."

"Why did you decide to come to this meeting with Sadhguru?" I asked.

"A friend told me about him," Robert said. "I thought it was interesting that a yogi would come all the way from India to talk with a group of American business people."

"What did you think?" I asked.

"He's really amazing," Robert sighed. "I've never met anyone like him."

"Yes," I agreed. "He seems to have insight on almost any subject."

"Do you meditate?" Robert asked.

"Yes," I told him.

"Have you noticed anything different about yourself or the way you handle things?" Robert asked.

"I certainly have," I told him. "There's a certain clarity that comes with it. When I need an idea or I need to make a decision about something, I have more control over my thoughts. I can see things more clearly, and the answer just seems to be right there. I know that sounds mystical and all, but that's what I've experienced."

At some point during our discussion with Sadhguru, he had talked about the clarity that comes as a result of practicing meditation. He called it "intelligence beyond logical thinking."

"When I say 'intelligence,'" Sadhguru said, "do not think of it as purely logical thinking. Logical thinking is just a small part of your intelligence. Right now, the body knows that when it inhales air, it should take only oxygen and leave out carbon dioxide. This is a huge intelligence, isn't it? There is enormous intelligence in our body which is constantly functioning. It functions even when you are sleeping. It will continue to function even if you go into a coma. It doesn't require you; it just constantly functions. When a body becomes diseased, it is because somewhere a certain part of the body's intelligence is not functioning. When the body's intelligence is fully functioning, it knows how to defend itself, how to clean itself, how to rebuild itself and so forth. This intelligence is built-in.

"So when we talk of intelligence," Sadhguru continued, "we are not looking at intelligence as logical thinking. We are looking at life; we are looking at intelligence as the means and the fundamental source of life.

"Everything in existence is hugely intelligent," he said. "Look at the earth that you walk on. Just see how intelligent it is. You plant a neem seed and only a neem tree grows out of it. You plant a mango seed and only a mango tree grows. Never does it get confused and produce a neem tree out of a mango seed or a mango tree out of a neem seed.

"So when I say intelligence," Sadhguru said, "I'm talking about the intelligence which is the very basis and the means of existence, and your aliveness right now. We want this intelligence to function on a higher scale. In a way, enlightenment means just that. The fundamental intelligence, which is the basis of life, is in full flow with you. That's enlightenment.

"So when we say intelligence," he concluded, "we are not looking at just being smart. We are looking at that dimension which makes life happen."

I believe this nonlogical intelligence that Sadhguru talked about is probably one of the greatest benefits from meditation. Having this type of clarity when making decisions is an incredible advantage in business. When you work with a group of people who have this clarity from meditation, they sense what is needed and complete tasks before they are asked.

As an example, I once volunteered for an advanced Isha Yoga meditation course that was to be held in a large rented tent. The night before the program, I was helping Jennifer set up lights and other equipment, while other volunteers were busy getting other things ready. Around 10:00 p.m., someone came running into the tent and shouted a very scary word: "Tornado!" Almost instantly, an intense wind hit the tent, and the tent support poles started jumping up into the air and pounding back down like pile drivers. People standing nearby had to jump out of the way quickly to avoid having their feet crushed by the leaping poles. Without any instructions, groups of people circled around each pole, grabbed hold simultaneously, and used their combined body weight to hold the poles down. As valiant an effort as this was, the wind was just too strong, and the center pole began to buckle at the top. With no other choice, the people holding the poles began to lower them, which brought the tent down on top of our heads. I crawled to a small corner where some sidewall supports were still standing. Rain poured intensely, as one by one the various meditators trapped under the tent made their way to the same corner as me. Twenty-five people ended up huddling there waiting for the storm to break. When the rain finally did let up, it was late, so we decided to regroup the next morning to survey the damage in the daylight.

I arrived at the tent site just after sunrise. Most of the tent was flat on the ground and covered with deep pools of rainwater. In less than six hours, approximately three hundred people would arrive to attend the meditation program, so my first logical reaction was that the program would have to be canceled. But the program was not cancelled, due to an incredible example of nonlogical intelligence in action.

Before I knew it, ten meditators had joined me at the tent site and were surveying the damage. Someone began using a push broom to sweep the water away. Another person grabbed another broom and began doing the same thing. Soon, there were twenty-five people there. As each person arrived, they looked around, surveyed the situation for a moment, and then went to work. Without any particular instructions, each person found something that needed to be done in order to repair the tent. Within an hour, there were well over one hundred people at work.

Slowly, the water was removed, damaged poles were excavated, and the remaining good parts of the tent combined to create a viable structure. By noon that day, the job was finished and the meditation program started without any delay. It was absolutely beautiful and amazing at the same time. I remember thinking that there was no organization on earth that could do a job like that. No business, no government, no army could do it, at least not without dozens of sergeants shouting orders. In our case, the clarity of each meditator took over and guided us through the process so that we functioned like one organism.

One of my favorite HR books, *Gung Ho*, talks about a similar incident involving beavers. When the beaver dam springs a leak, the beavers go to work repairing the breach without any particular plan. One beaver goes and finds sticks, while another digs for mud. Another beaver is there to place the sticks and use the mud to glue the sticks in place. Then off they go in different directions, as another group of beavers suddenly appears from nowhere with the same materials. They see what needs to be done, and they take action. They don't have to be told what to do, and no one has to manage them. I can only imagine what it would be like to work in a business among people who meditate and who have this clarity.

I met a guy named Michael at one of these advanced meditation workshops, and he was the first person who shared his story with me about what it was like to work with a team where several people were meditators. Michael is the CEO of a software business and was the first person in his company to begin meditating. After seeing the effect meditation had on Michael, eventually five other people with whom he worked also learned to meditate.

"What has meditating done for you in your career?" I asked.

"I'm a very passionate entrepreneur," said Michael. "I get very excited about what I'm doing. I put my heart and soul into the business. There is so much volatility in a start-up business like this, so I was having wild emotional swings. This was not only affecting me but also my team and my family. The biggest benefit that meditation had for me was giving me control over my emotions. I've always been a collaborative manager and listened to ideas. The number one thing is that I've been able to control my energy more. If a negative thing happens, I would typically get very angry and upset. Even if I tried to control my external response, such as what I said or my body language, there was no doubt that the negativity would ooze out somewhere. But after meditating, I still don't even have to try to control those emotions. If something not so good happens, I don't react negatively. It's amazing. It has improved stability and morale at the company, since the team hasn't had to deal with my mood swings."

"Did anyone give you any feedback?" I asked.

"My chief marketing officer, who I've known since childhood, said he doesn't recognize me," said Michael. "I'm that different in his eyes. I've also lost forty pounds. I very rarely drink alcohol, and I no longer drink caffeine. I used to be a coffee-in-the-morning and red-wine-in-the-evening kind of guy. But all of that has changed."

"What is it like to work on a daily basis with a team of meditators?" I asked.

"The person I work with the most is my cofounder," Michael explained. "He saw changes in me, so he began meditating. Our relationship is now very creative, fun, innovative, easy, and collaborative. We used to try to force our way through things, through any obstacles that were in our way. But now we have clarity from meditating that lets us know what is best right now. We have a lot more nonattachment to specific aspects of the business. I've had three people who work with my partner, Joel, tell me, 'Thank you, Michael, because Joel is so much easier to be around than he used to be.' He used to swear and yell a lot at employees and at customers. And now it is just like night and day with him. All of that negative stuff is gone."

"Has the business changed now that more of your team is meditating?" I asked.

"The story of the business is probably the biggest change that occurred because of learning to meditate," said Michael. "As I became more aware, the decisions I made and the priorities I had changed. We have a software technology that measures stress and emotion in the voice. We tried many different applications for it: insurance risk assessment, call center monitoring, consumer research, and entertainment. We were working on a believability meter that could appear on TV for politicians, athletes, and movie stars for interviews. It was an interesting business idea, but it became unattractive to me after I was meditating. I realized it was part of America's problem, the sensationalism of celebrities, and I just didn't want to be part of that. I wanted to do something that would help people. Instead, I came up with the idea to screen active duty military personnel for post-traumatic stress disorder, as well as to include our technology in the VA's suicide hotline. So, it was a dramatic shift in priorities of the business. Becoming more of a force for good in society rather than whatever it takes to maximize shareholder value. All of this has come at a time in the economy when things are the most volatile. Things have been tough for the business, and yet as volatile as things are right now, I've been absolutely calm internally through the past couple of years."

"That's amazing," I told Michael. "So, I assume you would highly recommend meditation to other business managers?"

"I think it is literally the single most important thing a person can learn in their lifetime," Michael stated. "And I don't say that lightly. It establishes a relationship with your true self. Before, what I had was a remote control relationship with my true self. Now, I have a direct connection. It affects who you are, then affects every decision you make, and every interaction you have with people. It is that deep and profound."

"What do you think about teaching meditation in a corporate setting?" I asked.

"It happens differently for different people," Michael commented. "Some people may be reluctant, because they don't know what it is. But I was lucky. I was ready for it."

"I think it needs to happen in as many businesses as possible," I said. "Corporate courses are already being offered in things like emotional intelligence and mindfulness, and there are corporate yoga classes. Meditation is a tool that should be available to everyone."

"I agree totally," Michael said.

I thought about the research I did on corporate yoga and meditation classes as I prepared for the business roundtable with Sadhguru. I found many businesses that had corporate fitness programs that offered various types of yoga , most of which were forms of hatha yoga that involve physical postures or the popular Pilates style of yoga that focuses on fitness. I did find a few corporate meditation classes with the primary focus of helping to control workplace stress.

Sadhguru has visited a variety of businesses around the world and, while speaking to corporate groups, he sometimes offers a simple meditation called Isha Kriya. It is a yoga and meditation practice that anyone can do, and it is offered completely free on the Internet at www.ishakriya.com. Recently, Sadhguru met with a Canadian police department and offered Isha Kriya to the officers in the audience. It was amazing to see dozens of police officers in full uniform sitting in their chairs with their eyes closed doing the meditation.

Meditators who have had some training sometimes offer lunch-and-learns in their businesses and play the Isha Kriya video as a way to teach their coworkers a simple yoga and meditation practice.

I continued my conversation with Michael on this subject: "Sadhguru has often said that meditation helps open up your nonlogical intelligence. It sounds like you've tapped into this in a big way."

"My clarity is improving significantly," Michael said. "Here's an example that is happening right now. A few days ago, I saw a tourism advertisement for Dubai. And I thought, that looks interesting; I'd like to go. The next day, my girlfriend was watching Tiger Woods at the Dubai Classic Golf Tournament, and I stopped to watch a bit of it. Then, I'm getting ready to take a trip to the Philippines, where we have a programming team, and I'm going with my business partner, Joel. Joel tells me, 'Oh by the way, I'm teaching a program in Dubai first, and then I'm going to the Philippines. Do you want to join me?' And of course, I had to say yes. I know now that there is something waiting for me in Dubai. I don't know what it is, but I'll figure it out when I get there. If you have this clarity of thought and are not attached to outcomes, but just try to align yourself with what feels right internally, and don't let the logical course of actions take over and talk you out of it, then amazing things can happen in your life."

After I finished my interview with Michael, I followed up with Robert, one of the managers who attended the business roundtable with Sadhguru. I discovered that Robert did eventually learn to meditate by taking one of Sadhguru's classes, and that it had a big impact on his health.

"Before I started meditating and practicing yoga, I had some health issues," Robert confided. "My job was very stressful, and I had to travel and meet with clients. I would be on the road, having dinner and drinks with a client, eating rich food all the time and drinking way too much. I started having high blood pressure and my doctor put me on some medication. I felt like I was too young for this kind of thing to be happening.

"After I learned to meditate and was practicing yoga on a daily basis, things started to change," Robert explained. "I don't know why, but I just suddenly lost the desire for alcohol. And, I just naturally started paying attention to my diet. Even when I was on the road, I found a way to meditate. Sometimes I would sit in my car in the parking lot and meditate before going to see a client. The same is true at work. Sometimes I lock the door to my office and meditate to clear my mind.

"The last time I went to see the doctor, my blood pressure was down to normal," Robert said. "I don't know how all this works, but it does. Maybe something changes in your chemistry."

I have heard similar stories from other meditators who reported that their migraine headaches had gone away, thyroid problems had been reversed, and hypertension brought under control. There have even been some medical studies that revealed that people who had suffered heart attacks and started meditating as part of their rehabilitation had a survivor rate that was much higher than those who did not.

Sadhguru had said that a person could unlock their energies through yoga, which in turn would bring better health.

"When we say 'yoga,'" Sadhguru had explained, "for many of you it might mean some impossible physical postures. Yoga means to be in perfect tune. When you are in yoga, your body, mind, spirit, and existence are in absolute harmony. When you fine-tune yourself to a point where everything functions beautifully within you, the best of your abilities will just flow out of you. When you are happy, your energies function better. Have you noticed that when you are happy, you have endless energy? Even if you don't eat or sleep, you can go on and on. So, just a little happiness liberates you from your normal limitations of energy and capability.

"Yoga is the science of activating your inner energies in such a way that your body and your emotions function at their highest peak," he continued. "When your body and mind function in a completely different state of relaxation and a certain level of blissfulness, you can be released from so much suffering.

"Right now, you come and sit in your office and you have a nagging headache," Sadhguru said. "Your headache is not a major disease, but it takes away your capability for the day. With the practice of yoga, your body and mind will be at the highest possible peak.

"If you gain some mastery of your own energies," Sadhguru said, "things that you never imagined possible you will do simply and naturally. This is the experience of people who have started doing these yogic practices. It is the inner technology of creating situations the way you want them.

"With these same materials that we use today to build huge buildings," Sadhguru explained, "people used to build only little huts. We thought we could only dig mud and make pots or bricks. Now, we dig the same earth and make computers, cars, and even spacecraft. It is the same energy; we have just started using it for higher possibilities. Every human being must explore and know this."

➤ **11** ◄

Effortless Living

I often thought that meditation and yoga could have a major impact on health-care costs in our country. Our company was self-insured, so we paid our own claims, and it was easy to divide the total cost by the number of employees. It turned out we were spending almost $9,000 per year per employee for health care. Of course, not every employee had yearly medical expenses that high, but, nevertheless, it was an enormous drain on the company. If only more people took better care of themselves, ate better, drank and smoked less, and exercised. Meditation and yoga would be a great start in the right direction.

One of the greatest benefits I experienced was a sense of calmness. Sadhguru had said, "Every day you invest a certain amount of time for your inner wellbeing. You start your day with this. Whether situations are going to be good or bad, situations are going to be easy or difficult, that's not the point. Every day you invest a certain amount of time for your inner wellbeing. If you do this, then you find whatever the situation that comes, there is no question of you working yourself up and saying hey, calm yourself down. Why? You are always calm. That's just how you are within yourself. You make yourself like that, then whatever the situation brings, you will go through it gracefully."

Robert told me that his overall health had improved dramatically since starting his yoga practice a year earlier. For the first time he was able to maintain the discipline of following a diet, which he did for over six months, losing over thirty-five pounds. He also made it a habit to go for a walk in the small park near the office each day just before lunch. All the little aches and pains that had been a part of his life seemed to all go away.

Sadhguru had defined wellbeing during the business roundtable discussion. "What is wellbeing?" he asked rhetorically. "When do you feel really well? Just look at this and see. Take the last twenty-four hours as a sample, and just see, when do you feel really well? In the last twenty-four hours, how many moments did you really feel well within yourself?

"If you look at this, you will see moments of happiness, moments of joy, moments of peace, are moments of wellbeing. Or, in other words, your wellbeing is fundamentally you being peaceful and joyful within yourself. So, if you know how to keep your body, mind, emotion, and your energy pleasant, if your energies are pleasant, you will be blissful by your own nature.

"Well-being will not come because you become the king of this world," Sadhguru insisted. "You know people who tried such things. They were literally sick. The great Alexanders of the world did not live well within themselves. If your whole idea of life is only in comparison with somebody else, if your whole idea of life is just about sitting on top of somebody's head, then you will never know wellbeing.

"Right now your wellbeing is subject to what's happening outside of you," Sadhguru continued. "You went out and somebody told you what a wonderful person you are, and you are feeling really well—top of the world. And you came home, people at home told you who you really are, and your wellbeing crashes in no time. You are just trying to bullshit yourself into wellbeing. And it has not worked. Your happiness, your peace, keeps crashing all the time.

"When your wellbeing is enslaved to external situations, you will be only happy or peaceful or well by accident," Sadhguru explained. "You cannot hold it through your life, you cannot hold it through twenty-four hours. Most people in the world do not know what it means to go through a twenty-four-hour span peacefully and joyfully. Something has to happen outside to make them peaceful or joyful.

"There are a million different forces which are creating the outside situation right now," Sadhguru continued. "All of it you do not understand. Only some of it you understand, and try to manage it to your benefit and the way you think it should be. And only to that extent it will be in your control. So if your wellbeing is dependent on what's happening outside of you, you being well, you being happy or peaceful, is a remote possibility.

"When you were little children, you were joyful by your own nature," he said. "Somebody had to make you unhappy. But today, somebody or something has to make you happy. The whole equation has gotten reversed. Because you are somehow trying to bullshit yourself into wellbeing. And it's not working.

"On a certain day, a bull and a pheasant were grazing upon the field," Sadhguru continued. "The bull is grazing on the grass; the pheasant is picking ticks off the bull. It's a partnership," Sadhguru said with a wink.

"There is a huge oak tree at the edge of the field," Sadhguru continued. "The pheasant looks up at the tree very nostalgically and says, 'Oh alas, there was a time when I could fly to the topmost branch of the tree. Today, I do not have the strength in my wing even to fly to the first branch of the tree.' The bull very nonchalantly said, 'Oh, that's no problem. You just eat a little bit of my dung every day. Within a fortnight, you will reach the topmost branch of the tree.' The pheasant said, 'Oh, come on. What kind of nonsense is that?' The bull said, 'Really. Try it and see. The whole humanity is on it.' The pheasant very hesitantly started pecking at the dung. And lo, on the very first day, he reached the first branch of the tree. Within a fortnight, he did reach the topmost branch of the tree. He just went and sat there, on the topmost branch of the tree, just beginning to enjoy the scenery. The old farmer, who was sitting on his front porch rocking in his rocking chair, saw a fat, old pheasant in the top of the tree, pulled out his shotgun and shot the bird off the tree. The moral of the story is, many times, even bullshit can get you to the top, but it never lets you stay there."

After seeing what meditation was doing for Robert, several of his coworkers also learned to meditate. Each of them also seemed to be transformed by the experience. Several of them joined us when I had lunch with Robert one day. They shared their experiences while we ate.

"I'm happier, I'm healthier, and I get along better with everyone," said Christopher.

"This process has enabled me to be more open to ideas," said Collin. "I'm more open internally with my employees and externally to what's going on in the world around me. And that has enabled me to not just see going from A to B, but possibly a bigger picture of what we need to be doing."

"When you are meditating, there's a calmness and peace about yourself," said Ralph. "It's indescribable and unspoken. I think that sometimes with all the technology we have and the way the world has become, we get wrapped up in talking too much and doing too much and not settling down. I think that becoming more meditative puts us in a position where we can say meaningful things and do meaningful things and leave out all the other things that are not important in our lives."

"I'm not always thinking about work anymore," said Karen. "When I'm at work, I'm focused. When I'm at work, I'm at work. But, when I'm at home, I'm at home. It's amazing. Sometimes I feel like in one minute I experience more than I experienced in an entire month."

What I learned from talking with this group was that all of these people credited meditation as the reason they were happier and healthier.

When Sadhguru had talked about the impact of yoga and meditation, he said, "The word 'health' comes from the word *whole*. When do you really feel healthy? When there is a sense of wholesomeness—your body, your mind, your emotion, and your energies are feeling in tune with each other, and you feel wholesome within yourself—that's when you feel healthy.

"Yet, a huge number of people are unhealthy," Sadhguru continued. "I'm saying even those people who are right now medically healthy, they are still unhealthy. They may not need any medication, but their system doesn't know any wholesomeness. There is no sense of peace or joy in them, so they're unhealthy. You think they're unhealthy only when they get depressed beyond a certain point, but I think you're unhealthy if you're not bubbling with joy.

"Your problem is you take one step toward ill health and you think it's okay," Sadhguru said, shaking his head in amazement. "Only when somebody takes ten steps toward ill health you think it's not okay. When you take the single step toward ill health it's not okay. So, there is no wholesomeness in terms of their internal composition of who they are. That's happened because they never paid any attention to it. This whole attitude of trying to fix everything from the outside has to go. No doctor or medicine can ever give you health. They can assist you when you have fallen into ill health. They can assist and help you out of it a little bit. But health has to happen from within you. And, health is not just a physical aspect.

"Today you know modern medicine is very much saying that man is psycho-soma," Sadhguru explained. "What happens in the mind naturally happens in the body. What happens in the body, in turn, happens in the mind. So, the way we are living here—our attitude, our emotion, the very basic mental state, the level of activity we are going through, how streamlined our minds are—all of this is very much a part of your health.

"So, if internally from within health has to come, we definitely have to do some inner engineering," Sadhguru said. "We definitely have to create an atmosphere where our body, mind, emotion, and energy is in good harmony.

"As there is a medical physiology, there is a yogic physiology," Sadhguru explained. "In the yogic physiology, we're looking at the body as five sheaths or five layers. There are five bodies, one inside the other: the physical body, the mental body, the energy body, the etheric body, and the bliss body. What this means is the first body, the physical body that you see, is referred to as the food body. Why it is referred to as the food body is because what you call as my body is just an accumulation of food. When you were born, this body was so small, but now it became this big only because you accumulated the food that you ate. So, what type of food you're eating definitely has an impact on what type of body you're forming right now.

"Are we eating the kind of food that is conducive for this system, yes or no?" Sadhguru asked. "Centuries ago people ate whatever they ate because it was a question of survival. But this survival became a culture of its own, and in each culture people started eating different ways because that's their culture.

"Now, if you look at the body scientifically and what type of food is most ideal for this body," Sadhguru continued, "yoga has many methods for seeing what kind of food is in tune with your body. If you eat food which is in tune with your body, the quality of your body will be good. But that's not the whole of it.

"There is a mental body," Sadhguru explained. "When I say a mental body, we're not looking at mind as in any one place. Every cell in the body has its own intelligence. Whatever is happening on the level of the mental body naturally reverberates through the physical body. Today you know if you have mental tension; you can get ulcers in the stomach, asthma in the chest, and cardiac problems. So, obviously whatever tension that the mind goes through naturally reverberates through the body. So, that's the mental body.

"The third is the energy body," Sadhguru continued. "In yoga, most of the work is on the level of the energy body. If your energy body is in proper balance, your physical body and your mental body will naturally be healthy. How can this be? Today I can show you thousands of people who have come out of chronic ailments that were generally considered medically as incurable but only manageable. They're off their medication. This is not by attending to the disease. This is just by bringing the necessary balance and cohesiveness between physical body, mental body, and energy body. If you bring this balance, the body will naturally be healthy and the mind will naturally be healthy.

"So, yoga is a way of bringing an alignment between your body, mind, energy, and emotion in such a way that the force within you, which is the basis of all this creation, gets to function freely," Sadhguru said. "Once this dimension functions, health is no longer an issue in your life. Physical and mental health will be well taken care of.

"People who have taken up challenging jobs in their lives must ensure they are well," Sadhguru continued. "If they don't know how to be well, they will spread their illness in their work because your activity is always an expression of who you are, irrespective of your intentions. With good intentions, you may be spreading disaster in the world because your work is always an expression of who you are.

"If people can invest about twenty-five to thirty minutes a day in the morning toward their inner wellbeing," Sadhguru urged, "toward certain simple processes, with which they can engineer their body and their mind to full health and wellbeing, there would be very little disease left in the world to handle. I would say that of all the disease you see in the world, over seventy percent of it is self-created. If you can invest this much time toward these processes, every human being is capable of living healthy and well."

All of my experience with yoga and meditation was put to a test one day when I was clipping hedges in my front yard. Using a small pair of pruning shears, I was trying to cut specific tall shoots on a camellia bush. My other hand was pushing some of the smaller branches out of the way, but somehow it got in the way of the shears, and I cut down on my own finger. I heard an odd crunch and instantly felt the pain. I jerked my injured hand out of the bushes and saw blood gushing from the end of my finger. I had accidentally cut off the end of my left index finger.

My wife, Jennifer, had been with me, so she led me into the house to the sink to clean the wound. When she looked at the extent of the damage, she said, "I think we need to go to the emergency room. This is a bit more than we can handle here."

There was no panic and no rush as we drove to the emergency clinic, but all kinds of questions entered my mind: Will I be able to use my hand? What are they going to do at the clinic? I don't like to see blood. Am I going to faint?

Jennifer must have sensed this and gently said, "Just chant."

Before my thoughts got out of hand and panic set in, I meditated to stay calm. A quiet stillness came over me that carried me through the next few hours as we checked in at the clinic and the doctors and nurses began their treatment.

After the wound had been thoroughly evaluated by the emergency room nurse, the doctor came in and spoke with me.

"Usually fingers will grow back if you cut them off before the last joint," the doctor said. "You'll even get your fingerprint back, but you probably won't have much feeling."

Later when I returned home with my bandaged finger, one of the first things I saw was the camellia bush in the front yard. Something came over me at that moment, and a voice inside my head whispered, "Finish the job."

I then told Jennifer, "It may sound strange, but I want to finish clipping the bush."

We both knew it was the right thing to do, so together we walked over to the bush, and I picked up the shears off the ground. I then saw the bloody tip of my finger lying in the dirt. I picked it up without feeling any emotion, dug a small hole at the base of the camellia, and buried the small body part. I then went back to work clipping the bush where I had left off and finished the job.

The doctor was right, and over the next few months my fingertip grew back, and over the next few years the feeling slowly came back.

I give credit to the way we both handled that situation to our yoga and meditation. Life does have its ups and downs, and it's not always pretty and pleasant; however, with the right tools you can decide for yourself how you're going to be.

➤ 12 ⬀

Meditating at Work

Just before lunch one day, I closed my door, sat on the floor, and rested my back against the wall. I closed my eyes, exhaled deeply, and slipped into my meditation. At first, the thoughts from the day's work were racing through my head, reminding me of deadlines, phone calls that needed to be made, emails that needed answering, and upcoming meetings. As the thoughts began to drop off, soon I was coasting along in a very relaxed state.

I normally meditated for about fifteen minutes before lunch, when I was a little hungry and a little tired from the morning's activities. My meditations were like short power naps that cleared my mind—like clearing off your desk. However, meditation is much more powerful than a nap. It enhances your overall capabilities.

Sadhguru had compared the mind to a dirty flashlight. "When you become meditative," Sadhguru said, "you will see, your intellectual capabilities will increase many times more than what they are right now. Not because meditation makes you intelligent, but because meditation clears up the mess—the muck that's gathered on the glass of your flashlight. As your meditation deepens, it clears up the muck more and more, and the flashlight becomes more and more powerful. It shows you things more and more clearly."

As I sat meditating that day, I heard a knock at the door. Normally, people knock and, if there is no answer, they leave. And, when I was in the middle of my meditation, I did not let phone calls or visitors at my door disturb me. For all intents and purposes, I was "out."

This time however, following the knock, the door opened and someone stepped into my office a few steps. Then, I heard an embarrassed "oh," and the person quickly exited and closed the door.

After I had finished my meditation, opened my door, and was back to work at my desk, a sheepish-looking Paula came to my door holding some papers.

"I'm sorry," she said. "I interrupted you in the middle of your...whatever."

"My meditation," I said, completing her sentence. "It's okay."

"I just have this report I wanted to drop off," Paula said, and then took a few steps into my office and placed the report on my desk.

"Is that what you were doing, meditating?" Paula asked. "I thought you were sleeping or thinking or something."

"Yes, I was meditating."

"How long do you do it?"

"Around fifteen minutes."

"What happens?"

"I use some techniques I've been taught in order to reach a meditative state," I said.

"What about all your thoughts?" Paula asked. "Can you stop them?"

"Well, yes and no," I told her. "I don't actually stop my thoughts, but rather turn down the volume. It seems like my body is here, my mind is over here, and I'm someplace else."

"I could never do that," she frowned. "My mind is all over the place. I couldn't sit still that long."

"I never thought I could either," I told her. "But with the techniques I learned, it became easy."

"I don't think so," she said. "Besides, they told me at church to stay away from yoga and meditation and all that eastern stuff."

"Why?"

"You shouldn't open yourself up like that. Something might jump into you."

I was shocked at what Paula had said, and I looked at her in disbelief.

"Paula," I said, "I think you know better than that."

The surprised look slowly faded from her face, and she nodded. She then smiled and left my office.

This was one of the main issues regarding the use of meditation and yoga in a business. Many people thought it was a religion or philosophy. As a member of the human resources department, I was keenly aware of the careful separation of anything religious from normal corporate life. Religious practices were tolerated, but anything that promoted one religion over another or any proselytizing was strictly prohibited.

Sadhguru had been asked at the business roundtable if yoga was a religion. He answered by saying, "Yoga is a science. As there are physical sciences to create external wellbeing, yoga is the science for inner wellbeing. It is just that, because yoga—as a science—evolved and was developed in the land of Indus, this civilization which grew on the banks of the river Indus, it was identified as Hindu. Yoga has nothing to do with any particular religion. It's a science for inner wellbeing. If you call yoga 'Hindu,' it is just like saying the theory of relativity is Jewish. So, from whatever culture or religious background a certain scientist came, you will not identify that aspect of science with that religion. Similarly, yoga need not be and should not be identified with any religion. It's the science for inner wellbeing."

I asked some of the business roundtable attendees about how yoga and meditation were accepted in their businesses.

"I do yoga and meditation in my office," Travis said. "But it's just me. We don't have anywhere for people to do it. All we have is a break room and some vending machines."

"We have a fitness center in my building," Kyle told me. "In addition to weight machines, they also have classes. They have two or three yoga classes a week down there."

My building also had the same thing. Our fitness center taught yoga classes after work on Tuesdays and Thursdays, but it was hatha yoga without meditation.

"Yoga and meditation seem to be spreading," Julia said. "A lot of people take yoga classes in various studios around town after work. Some of those yoga studios also teach meditation. I hear a lot of people talking about how much they enjoy the classes."

Leslie, a meditator I met at an advanced meditation course, told me that she was able to meditate at work, even though she worked in an open area where she didn't have any privacy.

"I work at a health care company," Leslie told me, "and they have a reflection room that is kind of like a chapel. They have a Bible and a Koran, and they have West marked off on the floor. I meditate in there. Only one time has anyone else come in. People know to leave you alone."

One of my coworkers, Jackie, whom I introduced to yoga and meditation, said that she meditates in her office. "Since I have a private office," Jackie explained, "I just do it there. I do it just before lunch. I told my colleagues what

Project Bloom

I was doing, so I would just shut my door and meditate. Everyone was curious, but they leave me alone. They are actually very supportive. My schedule is such that we have back-to-back meetings until noon, and then everyone wants to rush off to lunch. They've learned to wait for me for fifteen minutes. Meditation is like a daily maintenance. The changes happen slowly over time, but they are there. I had a friend who went out on maternity leave for three months. When she returned, she noticed how different I was."

Sadhguru had once taken a trip to visit some business executives at Google in the Silicon Valley. After speaking to some of the employees, they took Sadhguru on a tour of the building. They were very proud of the way the building was designed, so that a break room or restroom was only a few steps away.

"What about a meditation room?" Sadhguru asked.

"We have one!" the tour guide said, almost shouting with enthusiasm. He then led Sadhguru down to a remote end of the building, where a small room had been set aside for the practice of meditation. Inside, there were a few comfortable chairs, and some large overstuffed pillows on the floor.

After he left the building, Sadhguru later commented, "They had fifty rooms where people could take coffee breaks, but only one meditation room. At least it's a start."

➤ **13** ◄

Moving Mountains

It had been nearly two months since I submitted the proposal for Project Bloom. I had not heard anything, but I hadn't completely lost hope either.

One day when I came home from work, Jennifer told me that Sadhguru was organizing a trek through the Himalayas. She explained that the trip would require three to four weeks, and she wanted us both to go.

"It's a chance to take a journey with Sadhguru through the Himalayas!" Jennifer exclaimed. "It's an adventure of a lifetime. I can take a camera and shoot some amazing footage."

I have to admit it sounded incredible, but I didn't have enough vacation time for a trip like this. I was torn between wanting to go and the responsibility I felt to keep working. We had enough savings to survive if I quit, but something inside of me kept saying that I shouldn't go. I didn't know if it was fear and doubt, or something wiser that could see a bigger picture.

We still had several weeks to make a decision, so I waited. Jennifer started making preparations for the trip. She obtained an Indian visa and received the necessary vaccinations. She also started preparing for the hikes by walking through our neighborhood wearing a backpack filled with bags of dried beans.

Eventually the deadline for the Dhyan Yatra came, so I had to make a decision.

Jennifer was begging me to go, and she was going no matter what. I hadn't made any preparations, nor had I obtained the necessary travel documents and vaccinations. It was a tough decision for both of us; still, something told me not to go.

It was even harder to drop her off at the airport and watch her check her bags for the twenty-hour flight to the other side of the world. She later told me that she cried all the way to the gate. I cried, too, as I drove my car through the twisting turns of the airport exit.

I continued to get to work early each morning, and now that I had a private office, I closed the door and did my yoga practice using a small blanket and pillow that I kept stashed under my desk. Throughout the day, I would close my door, sit on the floor, and meditate. If it were not for my yoga and meditation, I'm not sure I would have been able to stand the disappointment of having missed the Himalayan trek.

I sometimes sat at my desk and daydreamed about the trek. I imagined traveling from the yoga center in South India to New Delhi, taking buses north to the foothills, through winding, one-lane mountain roads dug into the rock, until I reached a point where the buses could no longer travel. And from there, hiking to a mystical place called Kedarnath and meditating amid snowcapped, moonlit mountains. Sleeping in tents, in the stables of a thousand-year-old Sufi temple, and in motel rooms filled with spiders. Walking, climbing, and riding donkeys higher and higher into the vast range that contains the highest mountains on the planet. Dipping toes in the melting waters that are the source of the mighty Ganges River. Stepping over stones where countless sages had trekked throughout the ages. All of this and more were the visions that danced about in my head.

Sadhguru had talked about times like these when he said, "Desperation is of your mind, not of the situation. Right now, you are living in a wonderful home, but every break you get, you want to go walk in the mountains or sit on the beach. You want to do these things, isn't it? Now today you went home and you find your home is gone. It has disappeared. You have a wonderful opportunity to walk in the mountains, sit on the beach. But now you become desperate, isn't it?"

Sadhguru laughed. I had to admit he had an interesting point. I had a wonderful home, a job with a private office and a window, but I wanted to be walking in the mountains, the Himalayas.

"So desperation is not of the situation; it's of the mind," Sadhguru continued. "So, if you keep your mind in such a way that it knows how to stay balanced, or it does what you want it to do, when you face situations which are challenging—especially when you face situations which are challenging—it is all the more important that your mind functions properly, isn't it? That is the time when you really need to function sensibly. But that is the time when you are getting desperate. In desperation, your intelligence will not function well. So, situations are there. There are some situations you can handle. There are some situations you cannot handle. But there are no problematic or desperate situations. You must understand, this is the reality of life.

"You are not a superhuman being that you can handle every situation that you come across," Sadhguru continued. "There are some things you don't know how to handle and it's perfectly fine. It's not necessary you should be able to handle everything. It is just that you must be able to function to your full potential. You must be able to use all your capabilities and intelligence that you have within you. And that's possible only if you make some effort internally to see what you can do about staying peaceful and joyful every moment of your life.

"As we have engineered the world toward creating a convenient and comfortable atmosphere around us, we need to engineer our interiority to create a very convenient and comfortable way of existence within ourselves. If this is done, you will see there is no desperate situation. There are just situations. Every situation has something to offer. In every situation there is something to be enjoyed. There is really no such thing as a desperate situation. The desperation is of the mind. If your mind is becoming desperate, the situations are just quality control for you, to show you who you are. What kind of stuff are you made of? Situations will expose you."

I thought about Job from the Bible and how he was tested repeatedly. Many people of faith saw the trials and tribulations of life as tests of their faith. I thought it was interesting that Sadhguru mentioned quality control. Quality control, or QC, was an essential part of the software design process. The folks in QC would try to break the program and find any bugs that needed to be fixed. So, in terms of that analogy, the difficult times in life were a chance to debug your mind and find out who you truly are.

"It's not that because something happened, you have become desperate," Sadhguru continued. "You are a desperate human being, but passing off as okay because situations never really tested you. Situations expose you; situations don't make you. So your desperation is not because of the situation. Your desperation is because of a certain way of being within yourself. That's what you need to address.

"If you want to go out into the world and do many things, the first thing that you need to take care of is yourself. You should know how to keep yourself within yourself. Only then you can go out into the world and do what you want and come back in one piece. Otherwise, the world will break you. Once you have chosen to do many things, once you have chosen to increase the scope and play of your life, every day there will be situations that will leave you clueless as to what to do. And it's good. That means you are growing. If every day you are facing the same situations, that means you are stagnating, isn't it? Every day you are facing challenging situations means you are growing, you are going somewhere. You shouldn't be unhappy about that. Because that's what you are working for."

"The difficult times are quality control," I repeated to myself so it would sink in. New challenges and opportunities are indeed an opportunity for growth.

At work the next day, our HR department had an impromptu morning meeting. Mike's boss, Christi, the director of HR, hosted the meeting in a conference room, where she had ordered bagels, coffee, and juice. After everyone arrived and had taken their share of breakfast, Christi made an announcement.

"Sometime back we did an employee opinion survey for HR," Christi began. "And based on the results, we hosted a series of forums to solicit ideas to make improvements. From everything we heard, we've decided to implement three things that were suggested."

Christi wrote a large number "1" on the whiteboard and then, "MANAGER-EMPLOYEE INTERVIEWS."

"We're going to have monthly one-on-one, manager-employee interviews," Christi explained. "This will give employees a chance to discuss their ideas and needs with their manager privately and face to face. You can discuss your career goals, issues with the way you interact with your manager, whatever you want to discuss."

Christi then wrote a large number "2" on the whiteboard followed by "EMOTIONAL INTELLIGENCE WORKSHOP."

"We're going to do some development around dealing with workplace stress and team building by scheduling an emotional intelligence workshop," Christi explained. "The leadership team went through this same workshop during our most recent leadership retreat, and we thought it was something everyone in the department would benefit from."

Christi then wrote a large number "3" on the whiteboard followed by "DIVERSITY TASK FORCE."

"We're going to form an HR diversity task force," Christi explained, "to focus on employee development, recognition, and appreciation. We want several people from each HR department to join and develop a plan they can submit to the leadership team. From our department, I would like to recommend Kevin, Martha, and Denise. There will be a kick-off lunch meeting next week."

I looked at Martha and Denise to gauge their reactions. Martha looked like she had been sentenced to hard labor in Siberia. Denise looked back at me and smiled. She seemed to understand the opportunity that had just been handed to us.

When the meeting was over, I went back to my office and was soon joined by Mike who rolled his wheelchair up next to my desk. "Just promise me something," Mike grinned. "No flower arranging, okay?"

"Okay," I told him, and we laughed.

I sat down and looked out the window and thought about what had just happened. They had accepted the proposal I had submitted two months earlier for Project Bloom. I now had a vehicle to try some of Sadhguru's ideas for changing the workplace culture. I had turned down a once-in-a-lifetime opportunity to go to the Himalayas, but another door had opened with a different opportunity—one that would bring tremendous growth, both personally and for the people with whom I worked.

➤ 14 ⧫

Action for Rejuvenation

After Jennifer concluded the Himalaya trip, she decided to stay and spend some time in southern India to observe firsthand the humanitarian relief efforts that Sadhguru's Isha Foundation managed there.

One of the coordinators from the yoga center took Jennifer on a three-day trip to see rural villages that were served by Action for Rural Rejuvenation, a program designed to serve the rural poor. Jennifer took along a video camera to shoot some scenes of what she found there.

While the people in these villages were extremely poor and lived in huts with dirt floors that they shared with their livestock, they seemed very happy. Jennifer watched as an elderly woman in a tattered dress swept the dirt in front of her hut. While she worked, there were goats and chickens that walked in and out of the woman's hut. When the old woman looked up at Jennifer, Jennifer saw a vibrancy that she rarely saw in the United States.

"The woman was glowing," Jennifer later told me. "There were so many people like that. They were absolutely vibrant."

At one point, Jennifer was surrounded by many small children who gathered around her, each reaching out to touch her. Since the rural women only did domestic duties and rarely traveled, it was a major event to see a woman with a video camera, and a white woman at that. There were so many kids, Jennifer couldn't move. Dozens of tiny hands and arms reached out to touch her as if she were a rock star. The coordinator had to come to her rescue by prying away the kids a few at a time, until a small path opened and Jennifer could wiggle through it.

Jennifer stopped in the center of one deserted-looking village to talk with the coordinator and plan out some shots. One of the Action for Rural Rejuvenation mobile medical trucks had arrived and parked, and the doctor and nurse were setting up some tables around the truck. When Jennifer turned back to the village, she was astonished to see that several hundred people had silently lined up behind her to get free medical care.

In addition to offering free medical care, the Action for Rural Rejuvenation program also taught yoga and meditation, planted herbal gardens, and organized volleyball tournaments. Jennifer shot scenes of the yoga classes and gardens while the villagers were examined by the doctor and nurse from the medical truck.

Later, Jennifer interviewed several local villagers, including the man who served as mayor. The coordinator translated Jennifer's questions and the villagers' answers. The mayor told Jennifer that his village had seen a vast improvement after they started practicing yoga and meditating. Many of the men in the village had alcohol problems, but that had almost gone away. And the volleyball tournaments had imbued everyone with a sense of community. The village women, who previously didn't have time to socialize because of all their chores, were suddenly playing together as they hadn't played since they were children.

That evening, the coordinator took Jennifer to a volleyball tournament in a nearby village. When she arrived, she could see that the village had built a volleyball court with makeshift lights, so games could be played after dark, which was the only time of day when the villagers could take off from their arduous farming duties. Several hundred people filled the wooden stands. As Jennifer walked along shooting with her camera, she heard a loudspeaker making an announcement in the local Tamil language. None of it meant anything to her until she heard the word "Jennifer" followed by "America."

The game stopped for a moment, and everyone cheered and applauded their visitor from America. Jennifer was humbled by the experience and was once again surrounded by children. A group of teenage boys who had been drumming all wanted Jennifer to take their drumsticks and bang on their drums. She did this a few times, which pleased them immensely.

For the children in these rural villages, Sadhguru had started building schools. A total of six schools had been created that served over 1,800 students ranging in age from kindergarten through grade twelve. In addition to an education, the children are provided with proper clothing, footwear, and food. This program is known as Isha Vidhya.

The schools offer English-based computer education, complemented by innovative teaching methods. Sadhguru's intention is to eventually have 206 of these schools in each county (or *taluk*) within the southern Indian state of Tamil Nadu. When these schools are completed, they will serve over five hundred thousand students.

After seeing this effort in person, Jennifer and I decided to sponsor one of the children. His name is Victor and he's now seven years old. Several times a year, he sends us a picture he has drawn, while the school sends us an email copy of his report card.

Another of Sadhguru's programs that Jennifer saw while she was in India is called Project GreenHands. The project seeks to prevent and reverse environmental degradation and enable sustainable living by creating 10 percent additional green cover in the state of Tamil Nadu. Drawing extensively on volunteer participation, 114 million trees will be planted statewide in total.

As a first step, a mass tree planting marathon was held on October 17, 2006. It resulted in 852,587 saplings being planted in 6,284 locations across 27 districts in the state, by over 256,289 volunteers in just one day, setting a Guinness World Record. Since then, over seven million trees have been planted by over one million volunteers.

Back at the Isha Yoga Center, Jennifer interviewed Sadhguru about Action for Rural Rejuvenation. Sadhguru was seated in a garden near his home, with lush tropical plants and stone sculptures in the background. He was wearing his usual beige turban, along with a colorful blue shawl.

"Action for Rural Rejuvenation is an attempt to engineer the social situations which have gone bad, in such a way so that human beings can find a conducive atmosphere for themselves to blossom into," Sadhguru explained. "With the limited resources that are available in certain societies, how to make their life situations worthwhile, how they can find their full potential in whatever they are doing in their lives—that is the basic scope and aim of ARR, or the Action for Rural Rejuvenation project.

"This project is not just aimed at improving the economic conditions of the people who live there, though that is one of the major issues which needs to be handled," Sadhguru continued. "It is a way of inspiring a human being to stand up for himself, to raise the human spirit. There are many hopeless conditions there; economic conditions are bad; social conditions have slowly turned sour, and the environmental condition is becoming bad. If we try to fix all those things without raising the human spirit, it'll be an enormous effort which will go to waste.

"So right now, what I see is, if human beings are very spirited toward their life, they will somehow find a solution for everything," said Sadhguru. "But from outside, if you try to find solutions when human beings do not have the necessary spirit to put it into action or to make it a reality, it doesn't matter how much effort we put in, it will go to waste.

"So Action for Rural Rejuvenation is a comprehensive program to touch human life on all levels," he continued. "From health, hygiene, economic aspects, environmental aspects, social interactions—all this put together, a comprehensive program which is being put into place by dedicated volunteers in hundreds of villages in southern India. To create a necessary human spirit, and also a necessary social atmosphere for the human spirit to blossom and find expression so that they can create their lives the way they want.

"Everything is welcome," Sadhguru concluded, "in terms of physical help, in terms of financial help, in terms of people bringing different innovations into the village to make their lives easier and better than what is there right now. This can only happen out of people's heart. This cannot be done as a government project. This cannot be done with policy changes. This is one human being reaching out to the other."

When I attended the first meeting of the HR Diversity Task Force, I was thinking that we were about to start our own Action for Employee Rejuvenation. We were going to try to engineer a social situation that had gone bad, so that the human beings involved could find a conducive atmosphere in which to bloom.

Sharon, the HR Manager who handled employee relations issues for eight hundred people at the home office, served as our leader to get things rolling. Over a series of meetings, she led us through a process of brainstorming to determine what we wanted the organization to accomplish. I didn't tell the group that I had submitted a proposal for a Diversity Task Force.

The initial members of the team included two or three members from each of the four HR departments. Jeff and Tom were from the compensation department. Sharon and Carlotta were from HR development. Martha, Denise, and I were from HR information systems, and Susan, Dee, and Allie were from benefits. This mixture of people was the perfect microcosm of human resources. There were a few leaders who offered new ideas, a few fearful, unhappy people, and a couple of naysayers who proudly found what could possibly go wrong with every good suggestion.

Project Bloom

As ideas were listed on the whiteboard in the conference room, they fell into three categories: employee recognition, appreciation, and development. We discussed ideas that ranged from a department picnic to field trips to see various business operations. Other suggestions included lunch-and-learns, a book club, and volunteer projects where we could work together as a team on some worthwhile community project.

We also discussed a way to recognize fellow employees for above-and-beyond performance, as well as a quarterly newsletter for publishing those recognitions along with other department news. A variety of purely social activities were also discussed, including going out to lunch once a month as a group, organizing a craft club, and getting together once a quarter to play games while eating lunch.

I volunteered to take down the notes from the whiteboard and write the proposal.

Sharon then urged us to come up with a mission statement. After several rather lame tries, we came up with the following:

To promote the recognition, appreciation, and development of the HR team through direct involvement, exciting communication, and sharing of innovative ideas, which results in the fullest appreciation of the diversity of the team.

We continued to meet once a week for the next few weeks, going over the proposal and deciding on a final list of activities. Sharon kicked off each meeting with an ice breaker of some sort. Once, she brought a video of a motivational speaker. I asked if I could share a video of a motivational talk I had from the leader of a humanitarian relief organization in India. After all, this was a diversity task force. Sharon agreed, and I brought one of my favorite clips from Sadhguru's business roundtable discussion that had originally inspired me to propose Project Bloom.

I lowered the lights in the room, loaded a DVD into the conference room computer, and pressed the play button.

Everyone watched attentively as Sadhguru spoke on the large projector screen in the conference room. "If one forgets that whatever we are doing—whether we are doing business or politics or whatever—all this is being done fundamentally for human wellbeing," Sadhguru said. "All the commerce in the world is happening fundamentally for human wellbeing. At least, that's the intention we started with."

Sadhguru laughed. "So, if we think it's all right that in the process of doing business we can break people up, there is really no sense to it. Because every kind of business that we do in the world is only in pursuit of human wellbeing. If wellbeing is not happening to people, then there is no sense to business. And when you work together, when ten people or a hundred people or a thousand people work together, if they do not learn to be concerned about each other's wellbeing, then ultimately the whole business ethos will become such that the business that you are doing will not be of any wellbeing to the world. Anything that's not of any wellbeing to the world will not sell forever. It may sell today, but not tomorrow. Today you may somehow con people into buying it, but it will not sell forever. Only that which is truly of some value to people will be bought by people. People will invest their money in only that which is of value to them.

"So, if you are in a situation where people do just what they have to do to get by, where they will not reach out and do the extra things that need to be done, if everybody works like this, working in such a place is going to be extremely difficult. And it will be a life-taking experience."

I paused the video and looked around the room. Everyone was quietly stunned.

"When I heard that, I thought about this place," I said. "If everyone does just what they are supposed to do, nothing extra, then it will be a dull, meaningless place to be. That's why I think we have an opportunity here with what we're planning in these meetings, to do something more, that will make this a great place to work."

I then continued playing the last piece of Sadhguru's statement.

"Once you have chosen a certain line of work, you spend a large part of your time and life there," said Sadhguru. "If you don't create a conducive atmosphere for human beings to blossom, if human beings cannot be happy and joyful, their intelligence, their body, nothing will work well.

"Today, most of the business atmospheres have become like this—that just in the process of working, people are becoming so sick. So, whatever the success that you seek is actually a curse upon you. Lots of successful people in the world are not happy. Success should have brought you wellbeing. But, if it's not brought you wellbeing, then what is the point pursuing it? This is happening because of this attitude that you need not be concerned about anything other than business. Business is people. Your fundamental business is people. It's human wellbeing which is the basis of all the business in the world. If that is forgotten, then that business is of no relevance to human beings."

As the video finished, we turned the lights back up in the room, and everyone looked at each other for a moment until finally Allie spoke up.

"He's right on about most businesses being like this," said Allie. "The last place I worked was the same way."

"I've always thought you can't have fun at work," Carlotta admitted. "Work was work. It wasn't supposed to be fun."

"It doesn't have to be that way," Allie suggested. "I'm already having fun with this."

Sharon then told us that she had been asked by the leadership team to help us get started, but now that we had a plan, it was time for her to leave the task force. We would need to elect a leader.

"You just don't want to present the proposal to Samantha, do you?" Carlotta insinuated.

"No, that's not it at all," Sharon insisted. "This is going to be your team. You're going to run it yourselves."

"Then who is going to coordinate these things?" Susan asked. "I'm too busy to do it."

No one volunteered.

"Let's nominate someone," Carlotta suggested.

"Okay," said Tom. "I nominate you."

"And I nominate you back," laughed Carlotta.

"Why don't you do it?" Allan said, looking at me.

"Yeah, you should do it," said Allie.

"Let's vote," Denise suggested. "We have three nominees. Write your vote on a piece of paper, fold it, and pass it around to me."

Everyone followed Denise's suggestion and voted using secret paper ballots. When everyone had passed their vote to her, she counted each one and put tally marks next to our names.

"Okay, we've got a tie," said Denise. "Four votes for Tom, and four votes for Kevin. There was also one vote for Carlotta."

"I was the one who voted for Carlotta," Tom interrupted. "If it's a tie, I'll change my vote to break the tie."

"You can't do that," Carlotta protested.

"Yes, I can," Tom insisted. "I vote for Kevin."

"You just don't want to do it," Carlotta laughed. "You don't want to have to take that proposal to Samantha."

"You're darn right," Tom laughed. Then he turned to me. "Sorry, man. You're stuck with it."

The meeting ended, and I suddenly found myself leading this dysfunctional diversity team, exactly as I had wanted when I first proposed the idea several months earlier. It would help me grow personally, and I would be able to experiment with different aspects of Sadhguru's advice from the business roundtable and try them out in an incubator to see what was possible and what was not.

I gave my manager Mike an update on what happened and told him that I needed to get the proposal to Samantha. He took a copy and said he would pass it on. I figured I would get Samantha's feedback through Mike; however, a few days later, Mike wheeled into my office with a funny look on his face.

"She wants to see you at two o' clock today about that proposal," said Mike.

"Who?"

"Samantha," Mike said in a somewhat worried tone.

"Okay," I muttered, suddenly feeling anxious.

I remembered that someone had asked Sadhguru during the business roundtable, "Why do I get so anxious when a new project comes along?" Sadhguru had answered with his usual wit and insight. "The sense of anxiety in any human being is fundamentally happening because you're projecting the future situations based upon the existing reality. Whatever is the present situation, based on that, you are projecting a doomsday for yourself. It is a distress.

"If you know how to be at ease within yourself, every situation is an opportunity. The future is yet to manifest. Something that is yet to manifest, you need not manifest that in your mind and make a disaster out of yourself. That means there is room for creating what you want. What has already manifested, you cannot change that. But what has yet to manifest, you can change. But right now, there is no necessary stability in one's mind.

"This once happened," Sadhguru expounded. "A man was wrongly accused of a particular crime, and the king gave him a death sentence. He was to be executed the following morning. So when he was brought before the king, the man said, 'Oh King, if you give me a year's time, I can teach your horse to fly.' The king said, 'This better be true. Otherwise, you will be executed by being crushed under the feet of an elephant.' The man said, 'Okay. Give me your horse and a year's time; I will teach it how to fly.' He was given the time. He took the horse and went home. His wife was very distressed: 'What did you do? How are you going to teach this horse to fly? What kind of horse ever flies?' The man said, 'It's one year. In a year's time, the king may die. Or I may die naturally. Or the horse may die. Or, who knows, the horse may fly!'"

As the meeting time approached, I closed my door, sat on the floor, and meditated for fifteen minutes. I stopped thinking about the meeting, and calmness swept over my entire body.

I radiated that calmness as I went to the meeting with Samantha. When I entered her office, Christi, Mike's boss was also there. They both had copies of the proposal and had smiles on their faces.

"We just wanted to say good job!" said Samantha. "These are some really great ideas. I think they'll really help our department. Don't you think so, Christi?"

"I do," agreed Christi.

"There's one thing that we've been thinking about that is not in the proposal," I interjected.

"What's that?" asked Samantha.

"There's concern about how much time some of these things will take," I explained. "Some folks are worried that they don't have enough time to participate. Or, they don't want to look like they have enough free time to participate."

Samantha and Christi looked at each other and winced. "But we want them to participate," insisted Samantha. "Maybe we can offer an incentive of some type," Samantha suggested.

"That would be helpful," I responded.

"What if you come up with a points system and give them points for participating in different things," Samantha suggested. "Then, they can redeem the points for an extra day or two of vacation time."

"That would be great," I said, surprised that Samantha had suggested it.

"You and your team decide how many points to give for certain activities," Samantha continued. "Make it so that they need to participate in one or two things each month, and then they can take one extra vacation day every six months."

"Okay," I said, excitedly. "We'll come up with something and include it in the plan when we communicate everything."

"Oh, that reminds me," Samantha interrupted. "You know we've been having quarterly HR department meetings hosted by the leadership team. We do department updates, and we usually have a guest speaker from within the company."

"Yes," I said. "The speakers have been good."

"We want your team to take over coordinating those meetings," said Samantha. "You and your folks determine what we're going to do, and you can line up the guest speakers. It will give your team a chance to communicate things to everyone on an ongoing basis."

"Okay," I said. "When is the next one?"

"Sometime this quarter," said Samantha.

"Okay," I said. "We'll start working on a plan."

"Oh," Samantha said, remembering something. "Put together a budget for the things you want to do, and send it to me in the next few days. I've budgeted some money for team building and development, so hopefully I'll have enough there to take care of this."

Samantha thanked me for my efforts on the HR Diversity Task Force, and I left her office with an excited anticipation of the future. Everything was falling into place.

Sadhguru was right. When you have control over your mind and your energies through meditation, you can create whatever you can imagine. I had just witnessed that happen with the birth of Project Bloom.

➤ 15 ⤝

Full-Time Human Being

I kept the news of my meeting with Samantha secret until the next meeting of the HR Diversity Task Force. Unlike most business meetings to which everyone is prompt, the task force team members floated in fashionably late. I waited fifteen minutes until we had enough people in the room to get started.

"So, I had a meeting with Samantha about the proposal," I told everyone.

"And?" Carlotta asked expectantly.

"She went for the whole thing," I told them. "She loved it." There were instant smiles followed by a round of applause.

"There are a couple of other things that Samantha brought up," I responded. "You know the idea about incentives to get people to participate? Well, she suggested we give out points for each activity."

"What are the points for?" asked Martha.

"Extra vacation days," I answered. The entire room then erupted in cheers and applause. After everyone calmed down, I added, "We get to decide how many points to award and how to keep track of them."

The group discussed this for a few moments, as people suggested ideas ranging from certificates to printing our own currency. Eventually, we settled on the idea of certificates. When a person earned one hundred points, we would issue a certificate that would be signed by our Project Bloom banker. It would be redeemable for a half day off.

We looked at the activities we would be organizing and assigned points that would be awarded for participation. Most activities were worth ten points;

however, anything that required extra preparation time, such as hosting a lunch-and-learn or running an event, was worth twenty-five points. We decided our weekend volunteer projects would be worth fifty points.

"There's something else that Samantha asked us to do," I broached later in the meeting. "She wants us to organize and run the HR quarterly meetings."

A silent gloom descended over the room.

"That's a lot of work," complained Susan.

"We can all pitch in," Allan contributed. "Everyone will do just a little something extra and share the load."

"At least it will be different," said Martha. "I'll help."

"We'll have to find guest speakers and organize activities," I explained. "But, it gives us a way to communicate our activities and programs to the entire department."

"When do we have to do the first one?" asked Tom.

"Sometime in the next few months," I answered. "We'll have to start planning for it soon."

"I can probably line up a guest speaker," Tom said. "I can get someone from one of the new businesses to come and do a presentation."

"That would be great," I responded. "And we'll need some type of team-building activity."

"I hate team-building activities," said Martha.

"Do we have to do department reports?" asked Allan. "Those are so boring."

"Nobody cares about those," added Tom.

"We probably need to do them," I responded. "But perhaps we can do something more creative."

"If we mess this up," Carlotta warned, "there's going to be hell to pay."

"I don't think so," I responded. "This is a chance for us to experiment. Try things out. Do things we don't normally get to do."

"She'll give us just enough rope so that we hang ourselves," Carlotta sighed.

"Don't think like that," I urged. "It will all turn out okay, trust me."

"I sure hope so," Carlotta said. "I got assigned to this committee by my manager. I'm a single mother. I can't afford to rock the boat if you know what I mean."

I decided that my first meeting as the leader of the HR Diversity Task Force went pretty well, despite the negativity from a few folks in the group. I remembered that Sadhguru had talked during the business roundtable about how to handle difficult people.

"There is no such category of people as difficult people and not-so-difficult people," Sadhguru explained. "There's a category of happy people and unhappy people. Happy people are always easy to work with; unhappy people are always difficult to work with.

"Someone has become difficult because in some way he's unhappy. We cannot go about fixing every situation in life to make it perfect. There is no perfect situation. But we can do something for the internal wellbeing of the human being, where a human being will be happy by his own nature.

"You will see whenever you find a person in his happy mood, he is always a wonderful person to meet," Sadhguru continued. "He's always a wonderful person to work with. But, if you happen to catch him in an unhappy mood, then he's a very, very difficult person to work with. Every business, every corporation, every group of people who work together, who intend to work together, should create a culture of peace and happiness in the workplace. If this is to happen, this needs to happen within each individual."

Sadhguru then added, "So every business has to dedicate a certain amount of time and effort to offer the necessary tools, where a person is capable of creating an inner sense of peacefulness and joyfulness within himself. Only when this happens, slowly you will create a culture of peace and happiness. Once this happens, you will see, people will be easy to work with."

I could see from my first meeting that leading this group was going to be like herding cats. Each person had his or her own agenda and reason for being there. Some were there because they wanted to be. Others were there because they had been told to come. It was fairly easy to determine who was who.

To prepare for the next few meetings, I reviewed some of the things Sadhguru had said during the business roundtable about leadership. On a video clip I watched, a restaurant owner named Charles had asked a question. I knew from conversations we'd had in the past that Charles was having trouble finding reliable help. He asked Sadhguru, "What have I got to do in order to manage the people who work for me, so they do what they're supposed to, and I don't have to threaten them all the time?"

"One thing you need to understand is, being a leader does not mean being a policeman," Sadhguru responded. "If you want to be a good leader, you must be able to inspire the best in everybody around you. You cannot inspire people to do their best if you are just talking about give and take all the time. You cannot inspire the best in people if you do not get involved with the people around you. The best way that you can inspire the best in everybody around you is that people should fall in love with you."

Sadhguru laughed, but it was great advice. I knew he didn't mean to romantically fall in love; he meant to truly care for one another. That was missing from our business.

Sadhguru continued, "If people around you have fallen in love with you, they will always do their best. So now, what is the technology to make everybody fall in love with you?"

Sadhguru laughed again, as if there was a magic potion you could add to someone's food to get them to fall in love with you.

"It is not a question of how much you can do or cannot do," he continued. "If you, in every step, in every breath, in every activity that you do, if you make this a part of your life—that you exude love in every little thing that you do—then you show that you care. It is not that you have to do something in particular. You bring this into your heart. This is not an act that you perform in your office. You truly bring this into your heart that you really care for everything around you. Then naturally everything around you responds to you in the best possible way. And, if people do not respond to you in their best possible way, leading them is going to drive you nuts.

"If you have to lead unwilling people, then you are going to have a huge difficulty. After all, people have come to work because they want to do it. But in the process of working, people will get into each other's way so that much resistance will build up over a period of time."

I could only imagine that this was the situation in which Samantha and Christi found themselves. They were trying to manage built-up resistance, and no all-day team-building session was going to fix that. It was going to take a grassroots effort from the employees themselves to fix the problem. I realized that is why they approved the concept for the diversity task force.

Sadhguru looked around the room and continued, "We need to understand this. Every transaction we make in the world is like this. What is your profit is my loss, what is my profit is your loss. In everything there is something to give, something to take. Whenever situations happen in such a way that you have something to lose, if you are going to get aggravated, or if you are going to get unpleasant, then you will see when they lose they are going to get unpleasant with you. So, only if the lubrication of love and caring for each other exists, then losing a little bit, giving a little bit, taking a little bit, is not an issue.

"When everything becomes measured, logical, giving and taking, then friction is inevitable. Once friction happens and once resistance comes up in people, you cannot lead or manage them. They can sabotage your life in a million different ways. Even somebody who is just doing a menial job in your industry or business can so hugely sabotage your life. It need not be a vice-president of your company. He can be just a cleaner of the floor. He can sabotage your life so badly if he wants to.

"Unless all of them look up to you, unless all of them have some sense of love and caring for you, managing them is going to be a huge difficulty. So, this is not going to happen unless you exhibit that in every act of yours. And it cannot be an act. It has to be a genuine feeling within you."

Sadhguru paused for a moment and took a sip of water. He raised his hand and gestured to the audience.

"Now, this is not just about the people you lead. The most pleasant way for you to be is loving. It's not just about getting work done. The most pleasant way that you can be within yourself is to be loving. The most pleasant emotional state that you can have is love. So, being that way is an intelligent way for you to exist. If you are like this, everything works. It is not that work is a separate aspect of your life. Everything that you do is a part of you. Who you are is what you do.

"When your concern is only yourself, the other person also makes his concern himself," said Sadhguru. "When two people are working in two different directions and they are in the same place, this is going to be difficult. This is why workplaces have become such places of tension.

"Workplaces have become hugely taxing on human beings, because people are working against each other, everyone working for himself. If we do not bring humanity into everything that we do, then what is the point of living here? Or, a fundamental question is, do you want to be a full-time human being or a part-time human being? If you are a full-time human being, you will manage to your fullest capability.

"Every individual does not have the same capabilities," Sadhguru explained. "When it comes to outside realities, for each one of us, our capabilities are different. No two human beings are capable the same way.

"But, when it comes to the internal experience, all of us are capable of joy, all of us are capable of peace, all of us are capable of love. So the inner situations, if they are common, if all of us are happy and joyful, do you see that when you are happy, you are not in conflict with anybody in the world? No matter what, you are willing to go on with it because there is no problem.

"So, there is really no problem in your business or the world around you. There is only one problem—and that is you." Sadhguru pointed around the room at the individual members of the audience, and then pointed at himself. "If you solve this one problem, you will see, there is no other problem in the world."

➤ **16** ◄

Emotional Intelligence

Along with the HR Diversity Task Force and the management interview sessions, everyone in the HR department attended an emotional intelligence workshop. It was one of the three things Samantha and her leadership team had offered as a response to the employee survey and feedback sessions.

I knew emotional intelligence was a hot topic in corporate training circles, just like diversity, but I really didn't know any more about it. The class was conducted by a pair of industrial psychologists who explained that emotional intelligence was the study of how emotions affected our energy, commitment, and motivation. Our emotions determined how we saw other people, whether we liked or disliked them, accepted or rejected them, approached or avoided them.

At the root of it all was our personality. Our emotions were layered like an onion with the first layer shaped by our age, race, gender, and physical ability. The next layer included our marital status, religion, income, education, work experience, and geographic location. The outer layer was influenced by our job type, management status, seniority level, work location, and group membership. Dealing with individuals across these differences could trigger powerful emotional responses.

Emotional intelligence wanted us to look inside ourselves to find out what makes us tick. We needed to get comfortable within our own skins, and understand our likes and dislikes and trigger points. We needed to develop the skill of maintaining a positive attitude in the face of upsetting emotions. We needed to develop empathy toward others, so that we could look beyond our initial emotions and be more accepting of the differences between people. Finally, we needed to learn how to communicate effectively to resolve conflicts and build productive relationships.

The emotional intelligence workshop involved a variety of group activities that helped demonstrate the concepts. Everyone also got a nice full-color workbook with questionnaires and diagrams that were supposed to assist you in developing your emotional intelligence skills.

While I enjoyed the class, when it was over I couldn't recall many of the concepts. Needless to say, that meant I couldn't really employ any of the techniques back on the job. I realized that was the difference between these corporate training initiatives and a meditation practice. By practicing yoga and taking time to meditate, all of the onion layers of emotional bias fell away naturally. There was no need for workbook exercises or decision-making flowcharts. It just happened naturally without having to think about it.

Sadhguru had talked during the business roundtable about the advantages of having a purposeful personality. It was a personality that you created consciously—the way you wanted it to be.

"The word 'personality' comes from the word 'persona,'" Sadhguru said. "Persona comes from Greek drama. They used to use a mask to play a certain role because the same actor used to play multiple roles in the drama, so there are different masks here. So, you want to play a particular role, you take that particular mask, hold it this way with the handle, and speak in a particular way. So that's what a persona means, a mask. Personality means the mask that you are holding, got stuck to your face!"

Sadhguru laughed heartily. "To play a certain role, you put on a mask, and after some time, you're not able to take off the mask. That is a personality!

"You should have built your personality very consciously, but unfortunately for most people, over ninety percent of their personality is built unconsciously. It is molded by the situations in which they are living and they're exposed to. If one becomes truly meditative, one of the basic qualities of meditation is, it creates a distance between you and your personality. Once there is a distance between you and your personality, then you can make your personality as it is necessary for a particular situation.

"Your personality should be malleable, easily flexible, that you could make it whichever way you want," he continued. "If your personality is rigid, what it means is, you're wearing the wrong mask for the wrong role. Now, you want to play a certain kind of role in your life at a certain moment, you must be able to wear the right kind of mask to play that role; otherwise, the mask is useless. But right now, that's what has happened. Because of a certain type of exposure to life, you have molded yourself into a certain kind of personality. Unconsciously, you molded yourself so you are unable to take it off."

Sadhguru motioned with his hands to remove an imaginary mask from his face.

"So meditation is a wonderful tool with which you can unglue your personality from yourself, so that you can make this personality. If you were able to look at the mask once in a while, if you are able to see it from the front side that others are seeing, then you would keep it the right way as it is necessary for a particular situation in which you live.

"Your personality is not a permanent thing. It can change. You can change it every day, every moment. But most people are unable to change it because it was created unconsciously. But when life really demands it, people's personalities will change. When dangers come, when disasters happen, people will change their personalities. But it is not necessary for one to wait for a disaster to happen. If one is conscious, he can change his personality at will. That's how it should be.

"Marketing agencies are reading a certain type of personality into a whole generation of people," Sadhguru laughed. "This has some relevance because situations are molding people to develop a certain type of personality. So by looking at a particular situation for that generation, they are trying to read a certain kind of personality for an entire generation. It may not be one hundred percent true, but generally they're correct. And it's unfortunate that they're correct. That means people are not living out of their intelligence. People are being pushed by the situations in which they live. Or, in other words, human beings are not creating the situations in which they live. They are being created by the situations in which they live.

"When you say, I am a human being, it means that you can mold and direct the course of your destiny," Sadhguru explained. "If that is not happening, then the situations will mold you, not you molding the situations. When you say you are a leader, when you say you're a manager, fundamentally management means turning the situations the way you want them. Whether managing a business or managing a family or managing the whole world, what it means is, making things happen the way you think is right.

"So, if the situations are making you, then you are not a manager of your life. Maybe you are a manager in a company; but you are not a manager of your life. You must be the manager of your own life first. Be the manager of your own mind, your own body, and your own personality. Only then you can manage other people effortlessly. Otherwise, it is management by accident, not intent."

When I first heard Sadhguru talk about personality, it didn't mean as much to me as it did after I had participated in the emotional intelligence workshop and experienced its well-intentioned but ineffective approach. I knew firsthand that yoga and meditation offered the same benefits that emotional intelligence was preaching. However, when yoga was available in a business setting, it was usually a class offered in the corporate health club as a type of exercise.

Our corporate headquarters building had its own health club, complete with the latest exercise equipment, steam room, and massage tables. Yoga classes were taught once or twice a week, along with aerobics. So, one of the activities I coordinated for the HR Diversity Task Force was a private yoga class for my department.

Samantha requested that we integrate the emotional intelligence workshop into our activities for the HR Diversity Task Force. When we first discussed it at one of our meetings, there was little enthusiasm. Most of my fellow team members thought it was just window dressing.

"Let's have some fun with it," I suggested. "We'll do something creative."

At first there was silence. But, after a few moments, I realized they were thinking. An idea or two was offered, and then suddenly the room was flooded with creative ideas.

Eventually, the team decided to create a set of four color-coded keys. Each of the keys matched one of the emotional intelligence "key" concepts. Each person in the department would receive four of the same color keys. For example, I received four blue keys. As I interacted with my coworkers and witnessed a key concept in action that was represented by the blue key, I would offer the person one of my blue keys. The goal was to give away three of my blue keys, keep one for myself, and acquire the other three colors from my coworkers. When I had a complete set of four different keys, I could exchange them for points.

We decided to explain the concept to everyone at the HR quarterly meeting that we were planning. Tom had lined up a guest speaker, the general manager for one of the subsidiary companies. We also needed to do department presentations. Everyone hated the same old PowerPoint presentations each department had done in the past, so we decided to infuse the department presentations with some creativity as well. We came up with the idea of creating one graphical slide for each department, which we printed on precut felt jigsaw puzzles. We then broke up the pieces and put the various puzzles in separate plastic bags. During the HR quarterly meeting, when it was time for the department presentations, we would distribute one bag to each table and ask the people at that table to work together to assemble a puzzle. When they were finished, we would ask one person from each table to tell us what was on their puzzle. In the process, we would be giving our department presentations in a fun and unique way.

We also decided to use the HR quarterly meeting as an opportunity to announce the activities we had planned, as well as explain the points system and the vacation time rewards.

As we put the agenda together and decided roles for everyone on the team, I decided to mention one more finishing touch. "We have a nice mission statement," I reminded everyone, "but we need a better name."

The team suggested several different names. They laughed and joked and argued for and against different suggestions. It felt like utter chaos, but I knew eventually we would come to a decision. I listened quietly, occasionally making a comment.

Sadhguru had talked about the value of listening as a leader or manager. He had said, "You must be willing to listen. Listen to anything and everything. Somebody seems to be talking utter nonsense, but still you listen. Because most of the geniuses in the world spoke utter nonsense, as far as the rest of the world was concerned at that moment. It is only after a generation, people recognized those were the wisest things that were said.

"So if you are a leader, it does not mean you must know everything in the world," Sadhguru continued. "It is just that you are willing to listen; it doesn't matter who is speaking. Whether a child is speaking, or a great man is speaking, or a menial worker is speaking, or a manager is speaking; you learn to listen. It's very important.

"Learn to listen to life around you and the situations around you, very carefully," Sadhguru explained. "Only when you listen to everything around you, you have a perception of what is happening now and what's the next step to take. If you have no perception of what is happening now, if you take a step which is not conducive or not in accordance to the existing situation, then even if it's a great step, if it's not connected to the existing situation, it will go to waste."

So, I took Sadhguru's advice, and I listened and waited. Eventually, the team exhausted itself with too many ideas for a name, and no one could agree on any one choice.

Finally, I realized it was my opportunity. "What about Project Bloom?"

Everyone was silent, but then I saw a few nods, as they mulled over the idea. I then explained my reasons for the name. I told them Jennifer's analogy about the garden, and the different types of plants. I also pointed out how the name seemed to fit with our mission statement to recognize, appreciate, and develop the people in our department.

This started a debate between those who liked the name and those who thought it might be too cute. Even though 80 percent of the HR department was made up of women, keeping the principles of diversity in mind, they wanted to make sure the men weren't turned off by the name. Tom and Jeff both chimed in and said they liked the name Project Bloom.

To get a decision, I asked the group to pick the best three names and then vote. We numbered each name, wrote our choice on a piece of paper, and passed the papers to Denise, who had become our official vote counter. Denise unfolded each piece of paper and made tally marks in her notebook. When she finished, she looked up from her scribbling and made the announcement: "We are now Project Bloom!"

A week later, as I introduced Project Bloom to the human resources department at our HR quarterly meeting, I told them the story about where the name came from.

"I came home one day and told my wife that I had joined the HR Diversity Task Force," I said from the podium at the front of the room. "She looked at me and smiled and said, 'What did you do wrong?'"

Everyone in the department burst out laughing. After the laughter died down, I continued. "We came up with a new name that symbolizes what we're trying to do for each other. We're calling it Project Bloom."

I then reached down and unveiled the logo an artist friend of mine had created for us. It was a circular flower made up of little human figures, looking something like a dandelion.

We then took turns running the meeting, with other members of the Project Bloom team speaking and leading the activities, including the department update puzzles.

After we went through all of the Project Bloom-related activities we had planned for the coming year, we finally revealed the extra vacation time rewards surprise. There was instant applause from everyone in the department. A few people even stood for a standing ovation.

All of the team members in Project Bloom looked at each other proudly. We were suddenly heroes, and we were just getting started.

Blooming

The enthusiasm and creativity of the Project Bloom team continued strong for the next year. After seeing how much fun we were having at the HR quarterly meetings, four more people joined the team, which meant that fourteen out of the sixty employees who worked in HR were part of the Project Bloom team. The rest of the department participated in the activities we offered to the point that within a few months, we were awarding our first Bloom certificates, and people began enjoying extra days off.

Most of us worked administrative jobs where we processed benefits-related requests for health care, life insurance, long-term disability, and retirement. There was little opportunity for creativity until Project Bloom came along. Now, we had a chance to experiment, invent, and imagine. I watched many people gradually transform their attitudes and outlooks after just a few months. Difficult, pessimistic people began to loosen up. People took on new responsibilities and leadership roles that they normally would have never been offered.

Martha, who had always been pessimistic about the future, eagerly volunteered to lead some activities. She suggested we create a craft club, which became a popular lunchtime gathering. She taught the people who attended her meetings how to make jewelry, holiday ornaments, and pictures made from engraved copper sheets.

Melinda, another long-time employee who was known for being a no-nonsense person, joined our team and became our Bloom banker. She kept track of the points and distributed the certificates. She later told me that going once a month to deliver the certificates was the most fun she had at work for as long as she could remember.

"People are so surprised and happy to get those certificates," Melinda said. "You should see their faces when I hand them that piece of paper."

Allan volunteered to do a quarterly newsletter even though he knew nothing about desktop publishing. He quickly learned a few techniques from a sample template we obtained from the corporate communications department, and he published the first newsletter on schedule. Several others got involved in writing articles for the newsletter. They even brought a digital camera to work and began taking shots they could publish with their articles.

When we approached one of the managers, Tracy, to join our team, she declined the invitation saying that she was just too busy to come to our meetings.

"I'm in meetings all day, every day," Tracy protested. "But I would be interested in organizing a book club." And like that, the Project Bloom Book Club started and began having monthly meetings.

I kept remembering what Sadhguru had said about creating a situation where people could experience different responsibilities; the janitor becomes an engineer, and the engineer becomes an artist. Sadhguru called it loosening people up. That is what Project Bloom was doing, and it was gratifying to watch it up close in action.

One of the most interesting things about the project was how it gave people who normally had administrative jobs a chance to be creative. For some, their creativity was pent up inside them, and it came gushing out at first chance. For others, finding new ideas was a bit more difficult.

"Where do you get these ideas?" Melinda asked the group.

"I'm just looking for ways to have some fun with it," said Martha.

"I get ideas for things from looking at magazines," said Dee. "I see how the magazine looks, and I wonder if I can do something similar with the newsletter."

Sadhguru had talked about creativity, when someone asked him a question at the business roundtable about how to find inspiration when you had to be creative for a project at work. I remember being surprised by his answer.

"There is no such thing as creativity," Sadhguru had insisted. "Everything that human beings have done is only an imitation and modification on what is already there. Whatever machine you create, you will see the finest mechanical systems are already there in your own body. The finest electrical systems are there in your body. The most complex chemical factories are there in your body. Everything is already there. If you look at creativity in terms of art and other things, everything that you do is just a small imitation of nature. It would be derogatory to call this imitation, so people like to call it creativity. It's okay.

"If you want to be creative in any field, all you have to do is observe," Sadhguru explained. "If you develop a certain sense of observing every little thing that you do, every little thing that's happening around you, then you will see, you can be enormously creative in every little thing that you're doing. Creativity need not necessarily mean that you invented something fantastic. Just the way you sweep the floor—somebody's creative about how they sweep the floor; somebody else is just doing it as a mundane job. With every simple thing you can be creative, if you observe everything that's happening within you and outside of you. If you develop the means to truly observe what's happening within you on all levels of who you are, then you would be enormously creative. But even if you observe what's happening around you constantly, you will see there is always a way to do it in some other way, to do the same thing in a more innovative way. There is always a way.

"So creativity, if it has to happen, we have to develop an undistorted mind," said Sadhguru. "If you are carrying the baggage of life with you all the time, you cannot see anything the way it is. In yoga, we are always describing the mind as a mirror. A mirror is useful to you only if it is clean and plain. If it is undulating, or it has accumulated something, then it doesn't show things to you as they are. The nature of the mirror is such that this moment, if you stand before it, it carries you in full glory. If you leave, the mirror leaves you one hundred percent. It will not retain a little bit of residue of who you were. The next person who comes and stands in front of the mirror, it reflects that person in full glory. A million people look at themselves in a particular mirror, but these million people cannot leave one iota of their quality in the mirror. If you can keep your mind like this, the experience of life, the exposure to life, doesn't leave any residue on your mind, then you'll see things just the way they are. Then, there's room to innovate and create every aspect of your life.

"With my own life, I am supposed to be a teacher," Sadhguru explained. "But if somebody wants to build a building, they come to me. If somebody wants to arrange flowers, they come to me. If somebody wants to stitch clothes, they come to me. If somebody wants to lay their garden, they come to me. People in town have come to me because they want to build a bridge."

Sadhguru laughed for a moment and then continued, "Not because I have knowledge about these things in any big way, but simply because if I see something, I will see it so closely, I'll see everything the way it is. And when you see everything the way it is, how you want it to be becomes very simple. It is just a certain level of involvement that you develop when you don't make any distinction as to what is important and what is not important. Once you eliminate these aspects, of what is important and what is not important, what you like and what you don't like, what is yours and what is not yours—then everything that you see, you see the way it is, because the mind has the capability to do that. When you see things like this, it's very easy to construct anything, to create anything, because it is just a question of what material you have in your hands, and just how to put it together."

To apply Sadhguru's advice about creativity to Project Bloom, I made a little handout that I distributed to the team at one of our meetings. I wanted to encourage people to experiment and try job roles they'd never tried. My handout read as follows:

How to Bloom Creatively:
* Do something you haven't done before.
* Observe, listen, and imagine.
* Get your feelings out of the way, then innovate.
* Even the simplest things can be done creatively.

To maximize the pent-up creativity in the Project Bloom team, we divided into three committees with three or four people in each. One committee focused on employee recognition, another worked on employee appreciation, and the third worked on employee development activities.

To give you an idea of the magnitude and creativity involved in this effort, I've summarized the list of projects in each of the three areas.

Recognition

To recognize the contributions of fellow employees in HR, the team developed Bloom recognitions that involved an online submission system, newsletter articles, and gifts of flowers. When you noticed someone doing something extra to help someone else, you could go online and use the interactive form to submit a recognition note for that person. The interactive form emailed the recognition note to one of the Project Bloom team members, who was responsible for writing an article for the newsletter. In addition, the recognition coordinator purchased flowers and small vases and attached a small fortune cookie-sized piece of paper with the printed recognition to the vase. This little thank you was then left on the person's desk before they came into work.

I remember getting flowers and a few recognition notes myself, and they always brightened my day and gave me encouragement. After a while, everyone in HR had received at least one recognition flower, so we kept our vases in our offices in case another flower showed up unexpectedly.

As I mentioned previously, many Project Bloom team members contributed to the newsletter. It was published once each quarter and included a list of all the recognition notes that had come in the previous three months.

We also included a calendar listing upcoming Project Bloom activities, as well as articles and photographs profiling two or three employees. Whenever new people were hired in HR, the newsletter team would write an article about them and include a photo.

We also created a new-hire welcome package that was given to each new employee. It included information about Project Bloom, a copy of the HR personnel directory, some candy, and their first Bloom recognition flower.

There were two fun activities that graced the back page of the four-page newsletter. One was called "Guess Who?" It involved statements that described a particular person from HR. There was an online submission form where you could submit your answer and get points that could be redeemed for Bloom certificates. The bonus included a baby picture submitted secretly by someone in HR. If you guessed the identity of the Bloom Baby, you received ten points.

As an alternative, we created an activity called Pet Detectives. Various pet owners in HR would submit photos of their pet, which we included in the newsletter and as part of an online quiz. To get the clues, you needed to talk with your coworkers and ask around. This was an engaging activity that everyone seemed to like. I remember many times seeing someone at my door holding a printout of the pet pictures and asking questions like, "Found any fur balls lately?" I didn't have any pets, so my answer was always, "No, sorry, check next door."

Appreciation

The Appreciation committee's job was to find creative ways to thank the employees of HR for their hard work by offering fun activities that could be accomplished during lunch or after work.

One lunchtime activity was called Restaurant Explorers. It involved dining out together once a month at a different restaurant. One month it was Mexican food, then Italian, Chinese, Indian, and Thai. The goal was to dine around the world. Not only did we get a chance to enjoy good food and socialize with our coworkers, but we also got Bloom points.

To make it even more interesting, the coordinator of Restaurant Explorers created passports and rubber stamps for each country. After dining at a particular restaurant, you would present your passport to receive your stamp. Anyone who collected all the passport stamps received bonus points.

Once a year, the Appreciation committee also coordinated a department picnic at a local park. Project Bloom provided the hamburgers and hotdogs, and everyone brought a side dish. There were often activities that involved prizes and a chance to earn Bloom points.

To help us stay fit, the Appreciation committee also created the Weight Loss Challenge. Teams were formed with five people on each team. The winning team was the one with the greatest percentage weight loss. The Weight Loss Challenge lasted twelve weeks and involved working together to eat light at lunch, walking the stairs, and working out together in the gym. In addition to donating Bloom points for this challenge, Samantha's leadership team was so enthusiastic about promoting employee health that they contributed a cash prize of $500. The members of the winning team lost an average of ten pounds each.

To show appreciation for the members of the Project Bloom team, we had T-shirts made with the Project Bloom logo. They were a big hit, and the team members wore them on the weekends to some of our volunteer projects.

Probably the most popular activities coordinated by the Appreciation committee were the Bloom certificates and Bloom days. We assigned points for most Project Bloom activities. The recognition awards were the only thing for which we didn't give points, because we wanted the acknowledgements from coworkers to be genuine, and not to be inspired by points. The Bloom banker was a member of the Appreciation committee who kept the point totals in an Excel spreadsheet. When someone earned one hundred points, the Bloom banker would create a certificate and sign it. It was then hand delivered to the recipient. Two hundred points were required for a full day off. The limit was one extra vacation day every six months.

To take a Bloom day, you scheduled it with your manager and gave your manager the certificate. The manager then signed it to acknowledge that it had been used and gave the certificate back. Most people used their certificates as soon as they received them, and many kept the used certificates pinned to their bulletin boards like other awards they had received.

By the end of our first year, forty-seven people had earned a total of 12,840 points and earned ninety-nine half-day Bloom certificates.

Development

The members of the Development committee worked hard to find activities that would educate people and help them acquire new skills. One of their most popular projects was the Blooming Book Club. Membership was limited to fifteen people per book, so there was often a waiting list. At one point, we formed two book clubs because so many people were on the waiting list. Denise volunteered to run the second club.

The HR department paid for the books, and we alternated between business-related books and self-help books. Each book was read over a period of three months, with a club meeting once each month over lunch. The readers would share their opinions and talk about how the ideas in the book could be applied at work or home.

I remember reading books like *Gung Ho*, *HR from the Heart*, and *Rich Dad, Poor Dad*. In fact, the wisdom shared in *Gung Ho* was one of my inspirations for writing this book about Sadhguru's advice and my experiences with Project Bloom.

To help our fellow employees learn more about our business, we organized online activities and field trips. The online activities included scavenger hunts where historical facts about the business could be found by researching on the company's intranet and annual reports.

The field trips involved taking tours of field operations to see how the business actually made money. This was especially important for people in HR who had no direct interaction with the company's customers.

Another popular Development committee program was the lunch-and-learns. Attendees would bring their lunches to a conference room and listen to a presentation delivered by one of our coworkers or an outside expert. We learned about travel planning using the company's travel service, financial planning, Excel and PowerPoint skills, business and email etiquette, identity theft protection, email and file encryption, and how to back up your hard drive.

We also had show-and-tell sessions in which several coworkers would bring their vacation photos and talk about interesting destinations. By attending these luncheons, we learned about travel opportunities to Peru, Mexico, Europe, and Italy.

One of the lunch-and-learns that I hosted showed how to use Windows Movie Maker to make your own movies. For the demonstration, I put together a short movie using photos we had taken during Project Bloom events. The finished video, "What I Did on My Bloom Day," was a humorous look at what HR members would do on their free day off from work.

Several coworkers who attended this lunch-and-learn later decided to make a movie called "The Case of the Lady in Red," a mystery that featured everyone in HR playing roles in a detective story about missing data files.

For several lunch-and-learns, I played videos from Sadhguru and then provided a follow-up PowerPoint presentation with additional ideas. As an example, I did a session on time management that offered some tips on creating lists, prioritizing the items on the list, and scheduling time for your tasks. I then offered Sadhguru's advice on the subject of time management using the video projector in the room.

In the video, Sadhguru said, "Now, the division of time between family, work, and whatever personal life there is—how to manage this? There is no particular way to manage this, because different types of work need different types of time and involvement. And different types of families need different types of time and involvement. Your family may be glad that you are gone."

Sadhguru laughed, and a few people in the conference room sheepishly signaled agreement with their own laughter.

"Or, they may be longing to have you, it depends," Sadhguru continued. "And at no point can you one hundred percent satisfy either the work or the family or anybody. So somewhere, according to your requirements, you have to make a balance. This is the reality of your life: if you are doing this, you can't be doing that. You can only be in one place.

"Both in your workplace and your family, if you build that kind of relationship of trust and love, in both places, then when you need to make adjustments, when you need to go hard in work, the family will adjust. When you can go a little light in work and pay more attention to the family, the work will adjust. You have to create that kind of a situation, that kind of a relationship on both ends. Only then there will be room for adjustment."

Sadhguru continued, "If you have not built such a situation, the work will demand that many hours, the family will demand this many hours, but what to do? There are only twenty-four hours. So one has to build that kind of relationship, both in the workplace and in the family, where both are willing to do some adjustment because you are so precious. Make yourself so precious, both at work and family, that people are willing to make adjustments. If you don't make yourself invaluable, both to your family and to your work, then both of them are not willing to adjust. With the smallest aberration they want to fire you—or they want to divorce you! So you have to make yourself truly invaluable to everybody around you, that they can't do without you anyway. So they will adjust. This is an adjustment everybody has to make."

As I mentioned earlier, I organized a hatha yoga class in the company health club as part of Project Bloom. About fifteen people who had never tried yoga attended the class one afternoon just after work, including our vice president, Samantha. It was one of the only times she participated in one of our Project Bloom activities.

The instructor took us through a session that started with our sitting on the floor and eventually led to some standing postures, followed by a nice long rest at the conclusion with our lying flat on our backs. After an hour of bending and stretching, everyone was very relaxed.

Two other areas where the Project Bloom Development committee excelled were planning group activities at HR quarterly meetings and organizing volunteer projects. The HR quarterly meeting activities usually involved department presentations or activities to follow up on a workshop, like the Keys to Success activity that we did following the emotional intelligence workshop. The jigsaw puzzle department reports that we offered at our first HR quarterly meeting were soon followed by crossword puzzles and a Jeopardy game.

Besides witnessing the change of attitude and watching my coworkers bloom, one of the most gratifying aspects to Project Bloom was the volunteer projects. These events were organized on Saturday or Sunday and involved donating part of your weekend in order to help a worthy charity. We organized four sessions in one month to help build a Habitat for Humanity house. We volunteered for the Diabetes Association Tour de Cure bike ride, and the Multiple Sclerosis Society's MS-150 bike ride. One weekend a group of us volunteered to be ushers at the National Urban League Convention. During the holidays, we collected donations from the department and went on a $1000 shopping spree to purchase items for Toys for Tots.

One of my favorite volunteer projects was Project Open Hand. This involved working together as a team making meals for Meals on Wheels. We worked in an assembly line all morning on a Saturday to prepare and package over three thousand meals for sick and elderly people in the area.

One of the most controversial volunteer projects involved blood donation. Every few months, the Red Cross would come to the building for a blood drive. The first blood drive after we started Project Bloom, only three people from HR participated. One of them was Samantha. She had some trouble with the process and almost fainted, but she made her donation. Later, she came to me and asked me to include blood donation as one of our projects.

"We need more people from HR donating," she told me. "Give them points if that is what it takes."

I discussed this with the Project Bloom team at one of our meetings, and several people were adamantly against it. They didn't like the idea of bribing people into giving blood.

"They should give blood because they want to," Carlotta insisted. "We shouldn't have to bribe them."

"The problem," Melinda countered, "is that no one is donating. People need the blood. In some cases it is a matter of life and death. If we can offer someone Bloom points and that gets them to donate, then we need to do it."

For the next blood drive, we made blood donation a volunteer project worth fifty Bloom points. Seven people donated that time. That's four more pints of blood that probably would not have otherwise been collected.

In total, we had forty-seven out of sixty people who worked in the HR department participate in at least one program or activity. By the end of our second year, we increased participation to fifty-two people.

Project Bloom had started as an idea from Sadhguru during the business roundtable. He didn't say, "Go create a diversity program in your company and call it Project Bloom." Instead, he had said to find a way to loosen people up by allowing them to try out different jobs and responsibilities. He said to find joy no matter what work you've chosen, bring humanity into everything you do, dedicate a certain amount of time to create a culture of peace and happiness with your coworkers, and to set aside part of the day to focus on wellbeing. For me, all of that translated into Project Bloom.

When I decided to include Project Bloom in the book I was writing about Sadhguru's ideas from the business roundtable, I talked with several members of the Project Bloom team to find out how the program had affected them. I met with each person alone, usually over lunch, and conducted informal interviews.

When I talked with Martha, she told me that Project Bloom had changed her attitude about her situation at the company.

"Before, I felt stuck," Martha confided. "I didn't think anything good was going to happen for me. I had some health problems, my husband lost his job, so I had to have this job. I couldn't rock the boat. I couldn't go looking for something better. I just had to put up with the same old thing every day. But when Project Bloom started, and I was chosen to be part of it, I got a chance to try out some new things."

"Do you think Project Bloom has helped your career?" I asked.

"Yeah, I think so," Martha said. "I got to run one of the clubs. I pushed myself to make presentations at the quarterly meetings, and I got a chance to show what I could do. I even worked up the courage to talk to my manager about a supervisory role."

During the second year of Project Bloom, Martha was promoted to supervisor, given a raise in salary, and given one direct report. So her participation in the Project Bloom activities eventually paid off for her in a big way.

"What do you think Project Bloom has done for our department?" I asked.

"It has brought us closer together," Martha said. "I only really knew and talked with the people who had offices around me. I got to know almost everyone in the department. I used to think some of these people were just taking up office space, but I found out what they really did. It made me appreciate them more."

"Do you think morale has changed since we started Project Bloom?" I asked.

"Definitely," Martha said. "I think morale was pretty bad before. I didn't think the managers cared about us. They just cared about themselves. But letting us have Project Bloom showed that they did care. And the managers joined us for some of the Bloom events. We did volunteer projects together, and I got to know them better as people. I think everyone is a lot happier now. It's a better place to work than it was before."

Melinda, who was our Bloom banker and kept track of the points that were awarded for activities, was just a few years away from early retirement when Project Bloom started.

"I've worked for the company for over twenty-five years," Melinda told me, "and I've seen a lot of initiatives come and go. We had a diversity council ten years ago, but the only people on it were managers. It eventually just faded away, and they stopped having meetings. That's what I thought was happening again when Project Bloom started. I just didn't have any more enthusiasm for another program. But you guys were different. It wasn't a management program; it was an employee program. You guys started it, ran it, and came up with your own ideas. And I liked the things you were doing, so I decided I wanted to be part of the team."

"What did you get out of joining?" I asked.

"It's made me a better person," Melinda replied. "I wasn't much of a volunteer, but something happened when I volunteered to be part of the team. I enjoyed myself. So, when we had the various weekend volunteer projects, I volunteered. I thought it was great when we all worked together packaging meals for Meals on Wheels. And, when we took up the collection for Toys for Tots, I had a great time shopping for toys. We made a lot of kids happy that Christmas. I worked one cold February on a Habitat for Humanity house, painting baseboards all day. And, remember when giving blood was turned into a Bloom volunteer project. I had never donated blood before. That was my first time. I nearly fainted, but I'm glad I did it."

Project Bloom

Sharon, our HR manager, had helped us start Project Bloom by leading the first few meetings. She had then stepped down as part of the team to give us some room to figure things out for ourselves. Sharon was involved in the hiring process for new employees all across the company, so I asked her if she thought Project Bloom had any impact on recruiting and employee retention.

"I was talking to a woman who is new to our department," Sharon explained. "She was hired after Project Bloom was up and going strong. When she came in for an orientation after she was hired, she had all sorts of questions about Bloom. She said that when she heard about some of the things we were doing, she knew she definitely wanted to work for this company. As for retention, we haven't had that many people leave in the last year or so, except for one retirement and another person who transferred to a better job with one of the divisions. But, you know part of my job is helping mediate disputes between managers and their direct reports. Normally, I'll have three or four of those a year to deal with. For this department, after we got Project Bloom going, I've only had one such matter to deal with."

"How does that compare to other departments?" I asked.

"It is much less compared to other departments," she said. "I think it is a direct result of Project Bloom. Managers and their teams are communicating better. They're getting along better. That's a great accomplishment."

Tom had been a member of Project Bloom since the very beginning, when he changed his vote in order to elect me as the team leader. He was the only manager on our team when we started Project Bloom. He was also the one that Sharon was referring to when she said someone transferred to a better job in another part of the company. Tom had taken a new job as a director in the HR department of one of the subsidiaries. We still stayed in touch, and I dropped by his office one day to get his feedback.

"Do you think Project Bloom played any part in helping you get this new job?" I asked.

"Maybe," Tom said, thinking about it for a moment. "I did talk about Project Bloom during my interviews, and the management here had not heard about Project Bloom before. They thought it was very interesting and wondered whether it could work here. And, I guess they were impressed that I was part of the team that organized it."

"Do you think Project Bloom could work here?" I asked.

"Sure," Tom said. "In fact, we've been talking about it, and I've got a guy who is going to talk to you about it. He proposed something similar.

"That's great," I said. "I'll definitely share anything he wants to know."

I also talked with Tracy, the manager who ran the book club. She was not technically a member of the Project Bloom team, and the book club was the only activity in which she participated.

"I know I should get involved in more," Tracy told me, "but I'm in meetings all the time. I have a lunch meeting with someone almost every day, and a lot of Bloom activities are at lunch. I have to fight to keep the book club scheduled in my calendar."

"I didn't come here to bug you about that," I told her. "I just wanted to get some feedback from you about Project Bloom."

"Sure," she said. "What do you want to know?"

"Well," I began, "as a manager involved in a lot of different projects, and since you've been with the company for how long...?"

"Eighteen years," Tracy replied.

"...Been with the company for eighteen years," I continued, "I was wondering if you think Project Bloom has had any impact on our productivity as a department?"

"We don't really measure productivity like a manufacturing operation might do," Tracy said. "But I think we're accomplishing more in the meetings I attend than we've done in the past."

"How is that?" I asked.

"I used to have to referee a lot of arguments," Tracy explained. "You know, two or three different teams would have to work together on a project, and there were turf wars, misunderstandings about how a particular team worked, and personality conflicts. I don't see as much of that anymore. We know each other better. The teams are not so isolated. There's a level of trust that wasn't as prevalent before. I think Project Bloom has helped bring that to our organization."

Denise, one of the original Project Bloom team members, left the company before I could interview her for this book. She took a much higher level job as a director at one of the most prestigious hospitals in town. I contacted her sometime later, and we agreed to meet for lunch.

Over lunch, I told her about the book, the business roundtable with Sadhguru, and asked for her feedback.

"There are a lot of different ways to engage employees," Denise told me. "Project Bloom is probably one of the most inspiring employee engagement programs I've ever heard about. It's truly HR from the heart. We have something like it at the hospital. It's not called Project Bloom, and we don't do the same things, but we're trying."

"How did Project Bloom affect you personally?" I asked.

"When I decided to take this new job," Denise explained, "I was sorry to leave behind so many friends. Many felt like family. I think Project Bloom helped to create that family. And, that's an amazing feat in today's workplace."

⊱ **18** ⊰

Project Bloom Gardening Tips

When I think about the impact that meditation had on me, I can sum it up with two words: "Project Bloom." Much of what Sadhguru had said during the business roundtable had seemed hypothetical and idealistic to me. How could you give employees a chance to try out other jobs? How could you get people to try out leadership roles? How could you get employees to care about each other, to have fun at work, and to nurture each other? Somehow, that is exactly what Project Bloom ended up doing for us. In the process of starting and implementing this program, not only did I bloom, but my coworkers bloomed.

There were a lot of different things that we tried with Project Bloom that required specific technical skills. For example, we had a four-page desktop-published newsletter, online quizzes, and PowerPoint presentations. I knew how to do these things, but soon realized that not only did the workload need to be evenly distributed, but the team members themselves needed to acquire the skills as part of their development.

I asked for volunteers and took the time to train people and give them the software tools to do these projects for themselves. Some people bloomed and enjoyed their new responsibilities, while a few discovered it wasn't something they were interested in. The main thing was that they tried, and that they explored new opportunities.

Whenever we hosted our HR quarterly department meetings, we divided the presentations and activities, so four or five different team members had a chance to run the meeting and shine in front of everyone.

Sadhguru had said that a good leader is someone who leads from behind, not from ahead. "You must put the pyramid upside down," he had said. "A leader is somebody who is behind everybody, not necessarily ahead. Everybody should feel he is right there behind you.

"When people are leading armies, every moment is life and death. You're constantly making decisions about people's lives—literally life and death decisions. So, if you're a great general, you will not go and stand in the front. You will stand behind. Those who are in the front realize that you're constantly behind them, and that's what is needed in every field. So being a leader need not mean being on the top, or being in the forefront. It means that you're behind everybody. Only then you're an effective army of people."

This is what seemed to be happening naturally with our Project Bloom team. Because we didn't have traditionally set job roles, we were free to experiment and let as many people as possible try out leadership roles.

"When you are required to lead a team of people into some activity, it need not necessarily mean that you lead the activity; you just lead the people," Sadhguru had explained. "So if you want any work to be done well, it's extremely important that you spend a certain amount of time impressing on people the importance of the role that each individual is playing, and with what sense of responsibility he needs to fulfill that role, and what it involves in terms of doing something, and also not doing something, both ways.

"Also you must ensure that different members of the team don't get into each other's ways. So, if you want to go in a particular direction with as much speed as we can, it's important that we ensure that the different members of the team don't get into each other's ways. So, that is a leader's job, to ensure that they don't do that. It's like if you are driving a team of horses, you have to ensure that they don't step into each other's ways; only then you go in the direction that you wish to. So in terms of activity, in terms of actually doing work, generally the leader is given less work than others, because his job is to ensure that everybody produces their best. So ensuring that everybody produce their best, fundamentally depends upon how deeply you impressed upon them the importance of their role. Without that impression, you cannot get people to do what they're required to do."

When I originally proposed Project Bloom, I had hoped that it would become a company-wide diversity program that would engage employees and provide feedback to management. I envisioned becoming a consultant who visited field offices recruiting employees to join and form their own Project Bloom teams.

Shortly after our second year in existence, our diversity manager, Rose, told me that she wanted to document Project Bloom for the possibility of trying it out at one or two pilot locations.

"I've talked to some of the HR VPs at the divisions," Rose explained. "Several of them are excited by the idea and want to give it a try."

Rose had a consultant named Sandy work with me to gather content for a Project Bloom manual. Sandy took samples of everything, including the original proposal, our newsletters, and Bloom certificates. She also interviewed me to flesh out parts of the manual.

Around this same time, the HR department conducted another employee opinion survey. One of the questions on the survey asked to what extent Project Bloom was effective in supporting appreciation, communication, and development support for HR employees. Over 82 percent of the employees in HR responded with "Great" or "Very Great."

When Sandy showed me the finished product, I thought she had captured a nice snapshot of what Project Bloom was all about and how another organization could start a similar program.

Rose dropped by to see me one day and said that Samantha was going to make a presentation to the executive board about Project Bloom. A two-page summary had been prepared, and they wanted me to look it over and make sure it was accurate. As I read that two-page document, my mind leaped into the future, and I saw hundreds of Project Bloom teams working collaboratively across the country.

In addition to the formal efforts to spread Project Bloom that Rose had underway, several informal opportunities appeared. Gerald, the guy that Tom told me had proposed something similar to Project Bloom, asked to meet with me. He worked in Tom's divisions in the information technology department, and they wanted to form something called a "Fun Club." We had a long meeting in which I shared all the details of Project Bloom. He liked all the activities we had created, and he took a draft copy of the manual Sandy had developed.

Another opportunity for spreading Bloom seeds came from Susan who was part of the Project Bloom team. Her husband, Marshall, had heard her talking about it, and he wanted to get something similar going at the credit card processing company where he worked. He asked if I could come visit his company and make a presentation about Project Bloom. I took some of our materials and the Project Bloom manual and met with Susan's husband.

"So tell me about this Project Bloom thing," Marshall said. "It's all Susan can talk about."

"If you want to do something like Project Bloom at your company," I began, "you need to take the pulse of the organization. You need to do some surveys and focus groups like we did to find out if there's a need and if employees will participate."

"I think we need something like this, from what I've heard Susan describe," said Marshall. "But how would I convince management?"

"If you can get management to do some surveys," I explained, "and if the survey results come back with employees saying things like, 'No one appreciates what I do, managers don't care about us, no one knows what's going on in other departments, and there's no room for advancement,' then the organization has a morale problem. You might already hear things like this yourself in informal settings or around the water cooler. You need a real employee survey you can use to verify these feelings. Of course, you don't have to wait for employee morale to deteriorate to this level before considering a program like Project Bloom. I think everyone wants a workplace that is caring and focused on human wellbeing."

"So the surveys help get management buy-in?" Marshall asked.

"To implement a program like Project Bloom, management must be involved," I explained. "This program cannot be successful without their support. Approval might come from a department head, a general manager, or a regional manager.

"One key ingredient in Project Bloom is the points system to encourage participation," I continued. "With management approval, the points can be redeemed for additional paid vacation days. This was a bold stretch for our department head, but well worth the investment. You could consider other incentives, such as work-at-home time, company merchandise, or other informal employee recognition programs."

"How much does it cost to run Project Bloom?" Marshall asked. "That could be an issue here."

"It doesn't take much," I explained. "A small budget allocated for a program like Project Bloom shows employee appreciation from the company. While I've been involved in Project Bloom, our yearly budget for sixty employees has been approximately $2,000. We used those funds to pay for books for the book club, T-shirts, newsletter printing, and food for picnics."

"So, suppose I get management buy-in," Marshall posed. "What then?"

"If you get approval, the next thing is to create a task force," I explained. "The purpose of the task force is to plan and implement the program. To ensure that everyone is represented, you should have at least one member from each team or work group within the department participate on the task force. In our case, the task force became the Project Bloom team. Membership was a team-building experience in itself. To encourage participation, team members were given points for attending meetings and organizing various activities."

"What does the task force have to do?" Marshall asked. "Some people may be concerned that it's too much work."

Marshall listened attentively as I explained all I could about Project Bloom, and then he eventually prepared a proposal that he submitted to his management who ended up implementing a lite version of Project Bloom that built upon another employee engagement program they were already trying.

The advice I received from Sadhguru during the business roundtable meeting as well as my yoga and meditation practice were the seeds that sprouted Project Bloom.

There is a beautiful story I read on Sadhguru's website about a caterpillar that lived much of its life believing that it had come into being only to eat and sleep and do the rest of the things caterpillars did. However, it was unhappy. Somehow it sensed that its life had another dimension not yet experienced.

"One day, driven by a strange longing, it decided to become still and silent. It hung from the branch of a tree, weaving a cocoon around itself. Inside the cocoon, although constrained and uncomfortable, it waited, sensing and aware. Its patience bore fruit, for when the cocoon burst open, it was no longer the lowly worm that went in, but a beautiful, resplendent, winged butterfly which dazzled the sky. It soared and flew, no longer limited to its worm-like existence, but free and unbounded. The caterpillar had been transformed into a thing of air and lightness, magic and beauty.

"Once the transformation had taken place, it was impossible for the butterfly to return to being a worm. In the cocoon, the caterpillar had become one with its inner being and in this union it reached its ultimate nature. What happened in the cocoon can be described as yoga. Yoga is the path toward being boundless."

Whether you are interested in implementing a program like Project Bloom within your organization, or you are interested in truly transforming your work-life, I would highly recommend that you explore yoga and meditation. Sadhguru offers an online program that introduces you to yoga and meditation at www.innerengineering.com.

After this book project started coming together, and I had the wonderful opportunity to meet with Sadhguru again at his yoga center in Tennessee, I asked him a question about something that had been bothering me for a long time. I asked, "When I look around at all the misery in the world, I feel that humanity should be able to do a better job. How do we become better human beings, more loving, and more concerned about each other?"

"This is an aspiration that is there in every human being," Sadhguru replied. "But we are always trying to work toward it from the wrong end. People are trying to be loving. People are trying to be good. But, if you look at yourself, if I happen to meet you when you are very happy and joyful, I'm sure you are a very loving, generous, wonderful human being. This is true with every human being.

"But, if I happen to meet you or anybody when they are in a state of unhappiness, frustration, or some other sense of unpleasantness within themselves, that is when they could be nasty. So, there is no point trying to be loving, trying to pleasant to somebody else—when you are feeling pleasant, you are naturally pleasant to everyone around you.

"With morality, with ethics, people will always find ways to subvert these values," Sadhguru continued. "But, when a human being is feeling joyful, when he is feeling very pleasant within himself, he is naturally nice to everyone around him. So, my whole work is just to bring about that—to make human beings truly blissful because that is the best insurance we have."

I asked, "If enough people hold to these ideals, is it possible to influence society in a positive way?"

"Definitely yes," Sadhguru said confidently. "It is just that most of the time, belief systems are being passed off as spiritual processes. If you believe, 'this is it,' then you are bringing a certain rigidity into the very life processes that you are. Whenever you think, 'I don't know something,' you are very flexible. When you think, 'I know,' you become rigid. This rigidity is not just in attitude; this rigidity just percolates into every aspect of your life, and this rigidity is the cause of an enormous amount of suffering in the world. There is no such thing as a society; there are only human beings. Society is just a word. How human beings are, that is how society will be. So, creating human beings who are flexible and willing to look at things rather than being stuck in their ideas and opinions definitely makes for a different kind of society. And the very energy that each human being carries, will influence everything around them."

Project Bloom

19

The Making of a Manager

In the middle of my second year as team leader for Project Bloom, I was promoted and given the title Training Project Manager. In addition, my manager, Mike, moved to the benefits department, and I reported directly to Christi, the director that led our group. Along with the new title came various requirements, such as participating in company-mandated leadership courses that the company required of managers. Christi recommended that I enroll in several courses that focused on the legal responsibilities for hiring and firing employees, responding to harassment claims, and managing teams.

From what I experienced in the leadership classes I took, all of the leadership training seemed to require a robotic, emotionless approach. The company wanted all their managers to act the same way. It made sense as a standardized formula for business success, and for minimizing legal issues, but there was something very dehumanizing about it.

More advanced leadership training, which was made available for high-potential executives, required a three-day survival skills class in the wilderness. The participants were divided into teams and were forced to compete for food by going through obstacle courses, building their own shelters, and dealing with simulated wilderness events.

One of our department's managers, Elizabeth, had gone through the executive leadership program and told me about her experience in the wilderness of the Smoky Mountains.

"You had to sleep without a tent out by yourself alone," she said, grimacing. "I didn't sleep at all. Each day, we had these tasks we had to perform as a team. I was the only woman, and all these testosterone-driven men were competing with each other to see who was going to be the top dog. One guy would try leading, until his way of dealing with the task led us into a problem. Then someone else would take over."

The entire class was videotaped, and the videotapes were later studied by the participants in a series of classroom sessions, in which they analyzed their behavior under stress.

"That was the worst part," Elizabeth explained. "We had to go back into the classroom and relive the entire thing with someone analyzing our every decision. Why did you say that? Why did you do that? It was definitely a learning process. I'm a lot stronger because of it, but I'd never do it again. This job isn't worth what they put me through."

Sadhguru had talked about leadership many times during the business roundtable. Travis had asked, "Do you think people are just born leaders, or are they made?"

Sadhguru had answered, "Leaders are always made. Whether you made yourself before your birth or after!"

Sadhguru laughed so hard, his body shook up and down. He then continued, "It doesn't matter how, but leaders are always made. It is just that a certain person may have a certain charisma and a certain flair about his personality that he can lead a little more effortlessly.

"But people who lead with charisma can lead people to disasters. We want people who lead with good sense. It is not necessary always that the leader should be charismatic. You will see the greatest things in the world are being done—truly things of absolute human importance are being done—not necessarily by charismatic people. They are being done by sensible people who know what to do and what not to do. So this needs to be understood.

"Whoever you are, whatever you are right now, it is something that you have made," Sadhguru continued. "The only question is, either you made yourself consciously or unconsciously.

"You have manufactured yourself unconsciously, so you have come out as a mess—sometimes a successful mess, sometimes an unsuccessful mess. But, whichever way you are, if you have manufactured yourself unconsciously, you are successful only in somebody else's eyes. In your own experience of life, you will not be successful. Only if you have made yourself consciously, you are successful in your own eyes. This is very important—that you are successful in your own perspective. Not in comparison to somebody else. Not in a social perspective. So you will feel that you are successful only when there is fulfillment in what you are doing. When there is wellbeing in what you are doing, only then you will feel successful.

"So a leader is not only on top of the group; he must be on top of the world within himself," Sadhguru continued. "If he doesn't do something about himself, what he does with other people is going to be accidental, and any moment the whole thing can collapse on his head.

"So, leadership does not mean that you have to sit on top of a pile of people," Sadhguru explained. "Leadership means within yourself you are in top condition. And according to your capabilities, when your capabilities find full expression, things will happen.

"About capabilities, you know very well that for anything a human being can be trained," Sadhguru said. "Of course there are people with certain natural talent toward things. But even if you have a natural talent, that also is made by you—but unconsciously. So leaders are always made.

"If you make yourself into a conscious leader, it is better because you will function sensibly," Sadhguru added. "If you are just a charismatic leader, the charisma can be very intoxicating, both for you and others. And you can lead them to a disaster. Many, many leaders who could gather a huge number of people behind them, were always disastrous for the world. They led them into battles, they led them into disastrous human situations because they led just by charisma, not by sense."

The leadership training classes that I took focused on how to set expectations and goals for employees, how to coach them and offer feedback, how to track their performance, and how to evaluate success. I learned formula techniques for talking with employees, handling difficult situations, and settling disputes. One formula was three parts positive feedback for every one part constructive feedback. I could imagine some obsessive manager keeping tally marks in a notebook: *I gave Jane two positive feedback comments today. I'll plan one more for tomorrow.*

One peculiar aspect for me was that all the other managers who attended the training classes had teams that they managed. I didn't have anyone reporting to me, so I didn't have anyone on whom to try the formulas and techniques.

Our company had a peer mentoring program that matched two employees with equal job titles, so they could offer feedback and suggestions to each other about their careers. Each participant took a personality test and, based on the test results, I was paired with Carlotta, who worked as a learning systems supervisor.

Carlotta was in her early thirties and had worked for the company for seven years. She was in the training department, and her job involved coordinating classrooms, instructors, and training materials. She also managed the company's learning management system (LMS) for keeping track of employee training records. She had a job title of supervisor, and had one direct report, Sally, who assisted Carlotta with her duties.

During our time together as peer mentors, Carlotta confided that she felt like she was in the wrong department. Her work with the company's LMS was very technical in nature. Everyone else in her department was a manager or training consultant with limited computer expertise.

Carlotta once told me that her manager had asked for some help to find a computer file. "When I saw her computer, I nearly fainted," Carlotta said. "She had saved everything she had ever done on her Windows desktop. It was a giant mess of icons. No wonder she couldn't find her files."

Overall, the purpose of the peer mentoring program that paired me with Carlotta was to help us develop ourselves, as well as empower us to find innovative ways to help grow the business.

Someone had asked Sadhguru how you empower a group of people into taking a business where it needs to go.

"So, how do you milk the cow fully?" Sadhguru had paraphrased and then laughed heartily. "So how do you get the best out of someone? We need to know this. Only when the calf sucks its mother, she gives the milk fully. When you milk her, she will never give the milk fully. This is a reality.

"So, the people who work for you, if you treat them as your own children," Sadhguru explained, "they will anyway give their best. When you stop milking them, you are treating them as your own children, giving your best to every one of them; then they will do their best. There may be one or two who don't do their best—that's always there. Then, it has to be handled or you have to bear with them, whichever way. But, generally, a larger part of the team will give their best to what is needed to be done, if they see that constantly you have been giving your best toward their wellbeing. This does not mean you have to every day give them a raise. Just the human part of you—you're giving the best to them—they will give their best to you."

As Carlotta and I met as peer mentors and talked over the next six months, we became friends and shared our desires for the future. Carlotta wanted to get out of the training department and find a different job somewhere else in the company.

"I was originally working by the hour," she explained. "When they switched me to salary, I lost almost $10,000 a year of income. For the past two years, I've been trying to get them to fix it, but nothing happens. Maybe it is time for me to move on."

"Where would you go?" I asked.

"I've lived here my entire life," said Carlotta. "I've always wanted to live near water. My sister got a job in Seattle. Maybe I'll go there."

Ever since discovering the learning management system that Carlotta managed, I had been thinking that the company should have an online university. The LMS had that feature, but we weren't using it. In fact, we were only using this expensive system to keep track of our leadership courses, as if it were a teacher's grade book.

"Why don't we use the LMS for online courses?" I asked.

"The folks in my department don't want to have to deal with it," Carlotta explained. "It's just too much technology."

"I've been making various online training courses for HR. It would be great to be able to keep track of who was taking them."

"I know. We should be offering online classes in things like Microsoft Office. There's no training available. They just expect you to already know it, or to go take an outside class somewhere. We should be doing that here."

Eventually, the two of us wrote a proposal for creating a new Learning Services group that described how we could use the online university part of the LMS, and how we could develop online courses for the rest of the company. The plan included moving the LMS that Carlotta administered to my department, and moving Carlotta there as well.

I submitted the proposal to my manager, Christi, and she liked the idea and spent the next few weeks talking with Carlotta's manager, Janice. Janice didn't understand the importance of the LMS and was happy to see it go to Christi's department where it belonged. The only details were how to divide Carlotta's other responsibilities.

After a few months, Christi brought me in for a meeting to discuss the proposal. She told me that they had accepted the plan. The LMS was going to move along with Carlotta and Sally. Carlotta was going to be reporting to me, and I was being promoted once again to learning technology manager. I also received a small raise.

I felt a bit odd with the new arrangement of having Carlotta report to me because we had submitted the proposal together. But despite that, I left the meeting excited about the opportunity to start using the LMS the way it was intended. Many of the divisions were already using e-learning courses and would definitely become users of the online university if it was made available to them.

By the end of the month, Carlotta and Sally had transferred to Christi's group, and we had our first meetings to discuss plans for the LMS. During one of those meetings with Carlotta, she asked me a rather personal question.

"I assume that when they made you a manager, you got a raise?" Carlotta asked.

"Yes," I told her honestly.

"Can you do anything for me?" she asked. "I thought that maybe since I was transferring to a new department, you could look and see if my salary could be reevaluated."

"I'll talk to Christi about it," I responded.

"I'm just barely getting by," Carlotta explained. "I've got my son to take care of, and I'd really like to move. Our apartment complex isn't the safest. I'd like to buy a house someday."

The management training that I now had on my résumé had suggestions for how to put aside emotions regarding an employee's personal life. As you might expect, the company wanted management decisions based on good business criteria and not because one particular individual might be having some personal issues.

Sadhguru had some advice on this same subject. "Why we say do not bring personal issues into work is, personal issues involve emotions and things which need not be brought into the workplace," Sadhguru explained. "That is for the individual. You can tell an individual not to bring his personal issues into the work, yes. But now we are talking about somebody who is leading that individual. The person who is leading the individual must look at the overall wellbeing of the individual. If today for some reason, for some personal reason, the individual is down in some way, you can't get the best out of him, it doesn't matter what you do. Because, it's simply not within him to come out with the best when he is down in some way.

"So as a leader, if you are interested in getting the best out of him, you must be involved with every aspect of his life," Sadhguru continued. "To what extent simply depends upon what is your ability to be involved there. What is the scope for your involvement? But are you interested in being involved? Yes, you should be. Because if you are not interested in the overall wellbeing of the team, it's like you're driving a car, and you say, I'm only interested in the steering wheel, not in the engine, not in the wheels, or not in the gearbox, or something.

You must be interested in every part of the car, because otherwise the car won't function well."

The next day, I went to see Christi about Carlotta's salary. Christi told me that normally they didn't do raises except once a year, unless it was a promotion. I explained Carlotta's situation and how she had gone from hourly to salary and had taken a pay cut in the process.

Christi agreed that I could try and told me to talk with Sheena in the compensation department to get the salary market data on Carlotta's job. I went to see Sheena the next day and gave her Carlotta's job description to research. After a few days, Sheena gave me a salary report that showed that Carlotta was making about 20 percent less than the average pay for the same job in the market. This amounted to $10,000 less than Carlotta should have been making. The company's policy was usually to pay close to average as an effort to retain talent.

I went to see Christi about the next steps, and she said she would talk to Anita, the vice president, about the situation and see what could be done. After about a week, Christi told me that we couldn't get Carlotta a raise until January, which was still four months away. Anita said that it was against company policy to reevaluate salaries midyear, and we couldn't justify doing it for just one person.

I broke the bad news to Carlotta, but she seemed to expect it. Very shortly thereafter, Carlotta came by my office and turned in her resignation. She had already received a job offer in Chicago that paid $20,000 more than she was currently making.

I was shocked, but deep down I had expected it. "It looks like your dream of living near water is finally coming true," I told her.

Sadhguru talked about the responsibility a manager has in regard to employees. "Unless the leader takes responsibility of the overall wellbeing of the team members in every possible way, he cannot hope to get the best out of the team," Sadhguru had explained. "But how much you get involved with every aspect of their lives and their wellbeing depends on the nature of the work, and the duration that you would need to work with them. But anyway, if the time allows—if the time and space allows this—a leader should not hesitate to get involved with every aspect of their lives, because unless you ensure that all aspects of their life are going well, they will not do their best. There's really nothing which is out of the scope."

There was a going-away party for Carlotta that was supposed to be a surprise, but someone accidentally leaked the meeting invitation, and she found out. She did her best to act surprised when she entered one of the conference rooms and found it filled with her friends and coworkers. Most of the HR department and Project Bloom team members were there, and there were some going-away gifts. There was food and a cake, and Anita even showed up for a few moments to say good-bye.

When I got my first check in September, I opened the envelope and looked at the raise that was printed on the direct-deposit receipt. After taxes, the raise for two weeks of work amounted to a little over $200. The extra money would definitely come in handy, but it felt like it had come at a tremendous cost.

20

Work-Life Balance

With all of the changes associated with my new job and responsibilities for the LMS, plus the added stress from Carlotta leaving, I found myself working more hours than I ever had before.

I had to go through a long and complicated hiring process to find a replacement for Carlotta. A temporary contractor named Thomas who was filling in had the technical skills to do the job, but he had never worked with a learning management system before. Several other good people also applied for the job, but in the end I wanted to hire Thomas. So, I worked with Christi to come up with a job offer.

Just as we hired Thomas, our company acquired another company that was already using an online university and had over a dozen e-learning courses for new hires and sales training. They would be the first to start using the learning management system's online features, so I had to quickly learn how to configure the system for them.

After a while, a day would go by, and I would skip my yoga practice and meditation. Then another day, followed by another. I just didn't have time to meditate with everything going on at work. I would try to catch up on the weekend, but soon even that dropped off.

Sadhguru had talked about this very issue when someone had asked him at the business roundtable, "Sadhguru, where is the time for yoga in our hectic lives?"

Sadhguru responded by saying, "Now, you get up at six o'clock, go to the office, work, come back home, take care of the kids, eat, and till whatever time you go to bed, and you have a busy day. Where is the time for yoga? You have time to eat, to gossip, to work—you have time to take care of everything, but you have no time to take care of yourself.

"This attitude comes about because you try to act like a martyr all the time. 'I have no time for myself. I am giving myself totally to everybody.' What is it that you are giving? Your agitations, irritations, and anxieties are being passed onto children. If you are truly concerned about your children, creating a joyful and loving atmosphere for their growth on a daily basis, moment to moment, is more important.

"If you invest even thirty minutes a day into yoga," Sadhguru continued, "you will enhance your capabilities, and you will gain immensely, even in terms of time. The first thing is your sleep quota will come down. If you are sleeping eight hours a day, that means you are just sleeping off one third of your life. If your body and mind are more energized and active, your sleep quota will naturally come down. So if you gain three or four hours a day, just in terms of wakefulness, that is a huge benefit.

"Apart from that, with a simple process of yoga, your body and mind get more organized," Sadhguru said. "You would see that your level of performance becomes such that whatever you are doing in eight hours, you will very easily be able to do it in three or four hours. This is simply because, if you observe yourself throughout the day, you will notice how many unnecessary movements, words, and activities are happening in your life.

"If your mind becomes more organized," Sadhguru explained, "these unnecessary words and movements will disappear. Once they go away, you feel more energetic and will also have a lot more time. You have twenty-four hours to live each day. If we are organized and focused human beings, we can do plenty in twenty-four hours' time. If you are disorganized and unfocused, you think there is no time. Most people are not busy; they are just preoccupied. It is just too much preoccupation in the mind. If one makes time and brings yoga into their lives, suddenly the quality of their life will be very different."

In my case, I had chosen ambition over wellbeing. Instead of taking a short amount of time each day for my yoga practice and meditation, as Sadhguru said, I got involved in Toastmasters and soon became president of the club. I also became president of my homeowners association and began managing a major renovation project for the neighborhood. I also started a user group at work for all of the LMS users. Soon, there weren't enough hours in the day to take care of all my many projects.

Sadhguru had talked about the tightrope that a person walked between ambition and the desire to stay stress-free. "When you say you have an ambition, you are saying that you want to do something in a particular direction," Sadhguru had said. "So, if you are getting to do what you want to do, why should you become stressful on top of it? When you are longing to do something, the more opportunity you get to do it, the better off you should be, isn't it? Now you want to do something, if you get to do it you will become a mess. That's what you are saying. That means you don't have your systems in your control. Your body, mind, emotion, energy, nothing is in your control. You are living by accident. Your existence is by accident.

"The stronger your wanting is, the happier you should be when you get to do it," Sadhguru continued. "But in the process of pursuing what you want to do, you have become miserable, stressful, so you have to go to the mountain or the beach to feel peaceful.

"If you can be peaceful in the marketplace," Sadhguru explained, "if you can be peaceful in the most stressful, demanding situations of your business or your career, that is when you are truly peaceful.

"So peacefulness is not happening because of your work, nor is peacefulness being taken away because of your work," Sadhguru continued. "You are unable to be peaceful because of the way you are. Your mind is not taking instructions from you; your energy is not taking instructions from you; they are doing their own things. It is like you are driving a car where the four wheels of the car are going in four different directions, but you are planning to go somewhere. You will not go anywhere.

"So, ambition means you want to go somewhere," Sadhguru summarized. "And if you are getting to go there, why would you be disturbed? You are not getting to go there because the vehicle that you are driving is not in your control. You have to take charge of that. The whole process of yoga is just this— taking charge of all the faculties within you in such a way that you'll drive your body, your mind, your emotion, and your energies just the way you want it."

Without my yoga and meditation practice, within a few short weeks, I had gone from feeling like I was on top of the world to feeling depressed and anxious. I had so many projects going that I didn't take time to consider the people with whom I was working. I was focused on my needs as a manager, not the needs of my team. I started barking orders and snapping at people when problems occurred. I began to feed my anxiety in the company cafeteria and gained twenty pounds of unhealthy weight. I was definitely spinning out of control.

I could tell I was sinking into a depression and knew I should return to my yoga and meditation for therapy, but I became so depressed I didn't want to do anything. I let my work pile up, didn't return phone calls, and didn't answer my emails.

In the evenings when I returned home to my wife, Jennifer, all I wanted to do was sleep. I was so tired I would just flop on the sofa as soon as I got home and end up sleeping there all night.

During the business roundtable, someone had asked for advice regarding their own bouts of depression. Sadhguru had responded by saying, "The human mind is becoming depressed, simply because it has gotten lost in the logical dimension of the mind. Your intelligence says one thing, but the logical thinking says something else altogether. If you look at your life's experience, one little thing you feel, 'Oh, it's really worth living.' But, if you think logically, 'Is this life worth living?'

"Let's apply logic to its ultimate end in your life," Sadhguru said. "Imagine you wake up one morning lying down in your bed and you think one hundred percent logically. You don't look at your life's experiences. Do not think about the sunrise. Do not look at the birds in the sky. Do not think of your child's face, or the flowers blooming in your garden, or anything. Just think logically.

"Now you actually have to get up," said Sadhguru. "That's not a small feat. Then you have to go to the toilet, and then brush your teeth, and then eat, go to work, eat, work, eat, sleep. The next morning, it's the same thing. The next thirty, forty, fifty years, you have to do the same things every day. Think logically, one hundred percent logically. Is it worth living? That's why you become depressed.

"You think depression is natural," Sadhguru said, shaking his head in disbelief. "Once you declare that depression is a natural process, what is the way out? There is no way out. See, when you were born, as a child what was natural to you? For most human beings, except a few rare ones, to be joyful was natural. So do not declare that depression is natural.

"To be unhealthy, to be depressed, to be joyless," Sadhguru continued, "maybe you have a large company with you; you have the majority with you; but still it doesn't make it right or a natural thing. It doesn't make it effervescent with life. That is not the way of life; it is the way of the mind."

Sadhguru paused for a moment and looked around the room compassionately. He then added, "If you allow life to live, life is always exuberant. Just see everywhere—everywhere whether it is a plant, or an animal, or a worm, or whatever—just see with how much intensity life is going on in the world. Just dig under the lawn and see how much is happening. Is there anybody depressed out there? There's tremendous enthusiasm.

"Look at the little grass," Sadhguru said spreading his hands out around himself. "Uproot it and see. Just see the kind of enthusiasm that has gone into the root system. You put one little plant in a little mud and nothing else. From there it will just keep two leaves for survival. It will put one root down for over twenty-five meters. Do you think it ever gets frustrated? Life energy knows no frustration.

"It is a limited mind which knows frustration," Sadhguru explained. "because the limited mind works out of expectations, false expectations. When your expectations are not in line with life as such, or when they are fanciful psychology, then when it doesn't get fulfilled, the mind feels this is the end of the world.

"So getting frustrated is purely a psychological phenomenon," Sadhguru continued. "Just close your mouth and hold your nose for two minutes and see; the life within you doesn't say let me die. It says let me live.

"So anything that you do against your own life is simply ignorance and stupidity," Sadhguru insisted. "But right now you have gotten yourself into a mental state where you begin to work against your own life. Frustration, discouragement, depression means just this: you are working against your own life. But now, depression has become celebrated around the world—intelligent people must be depressed. If you don't have any depression, you are not intelligent. It's almost coming to this. I would say only if you are stupid, will you get depressed. If you are intelligent, how would you be depressed? Where is the room for depression? Only because you have put your intelligence on freeze, there is room for depression; otherwise, there is no question of depression or frustration.

"This happened in Martin Luther's life in the 1300s," Sadhguru recalled. "One day because all his efforts had gone to waste, Martin Luther was totally discouraged and depressed and was sitting in great sadness and depression. His wife was a very intelligent woman. She saw his condition, and then she went into the bedroom and put on dark black mourning clothes and then came and stood before him. Martin Luther looked at her and said, 'Why are you wearing black clothes like this?' She said, 'God is dead.' He said, 'What? How can God die? God is not dead.' But she insisted, 'No, God is dead. That is why I am mourning.' Martin Luther was perplexed. 'No, that's not possible,' he said. So, finally his wife explained. 'If you believe God is not dead, why are you sitting so depressed? Before you came into this world, everything was going fine. After you go, everything will go on fine. When you are here, why don't you just do your best? That's all you can do.'"

Even though I listened to all this great advice from Sadhguru at the business roundtable, I still found a way to sink into the depths of despair, anxiety, and anger.

One evening on the commute home, a guy in an SUV cut me off suddenly. The SUV was weaving in and out of the lanes, trying to get home a bit faster than everyone else. I was suddenly furious at him for violating my rights as a motorist and was determined to teach him a lesson. I wanted to catch up to him and force him off the road, so I began driving just like the other guy. The rage was building to such an extreme that I was screaming through the windshield at the other driver.

Suddenly, all of the cars in front of me slammed on their brakes. The domino effect of flashing rear lights caused me to snap out of my rage, as I slammed down hard on my brake pedal and screeched to a stop just a few inches from the car in front of me. Somehow, I had avoided the collision, but then I looked in my rearview mirror and saw a large truck speeding toward me, its wheels locked in a smoke-producing skid. I braced for the terrible impact, but it didn't come. The truck managed to stop without hitting my car. The front grill and the words FREIGHTLINER completely filled my rearview mirror.

I had definitely reacted to this SUV incident rather than responded. I'm sure that if I had still been doing my yoga and meditating, I would not have been affected so much by someone else's driving. I was lucky that the episode hadn't turned into a disaster.

Why we react to situations like we do was a topic that Sadhguru broached at the business roundtable. One of the attendees, Lenny, who was not a meditator, had asked, "Sometimes things happen and I just fly off the handle. I can't seem to control my reactions. I instantly get angry and want to lash out at the person. I don't know why it keeps happening."

Sadhguru took a long look at Lenny like he was seeing right through him. After a long uncomfortable pause, Sadhguru finally said, "For most of you, most of your reactions are just helpless reactions. Many times you tell yourself, next time I should not react like this. But the next time your reaction gets even more violent. This is happening, isn't it?"

"Yes, it is," said Lenny.

"Especially when you go telling yourself I don't want to react, I don't want to react," Sadhguru continued. "You become a total reaction. First of all, why are you reacting? What is the basis of the reaction?"

"I guess I'm carrying some anger around," Lenny said.

"This reaction is there in you fundamentally because you're still a collection of people," Sadhguru explained. "Please see that you're not an individual; you're a collection of people operating up there in your mind. When you're not an individual, you're naturally a reaction, because everything that you have within you is something that you have received from outside. Please look sincerely at everything you know as myself—your beliefs, your opinions, your likes, your dislikes; everything has been gathered from outside. Even your idea of what is beautiful and what's good has been received from outside.

"So, the first thing to do is remove yourself with everything that you're not," Sadhguru insisted. "You must see that you are not this or that. One day just sit by yourself and strip yourself of everything you're identified with piece by piece— your education, ideology, home, family, and even your body. Something so tremendous will happen if you do this successfully, and, of course, you will no longer be a reaction.

"This may not be a possibility for everyone," Sadhguru said, looking at Lenny.

"Why not?" Lenny asked.

"Some people need to be supported physically, emotionally, and energy-wise," Sadhguru explained. "So, there's an integrated practice that involves their energy, body, emotion, and mind. This combination works much better. But, if you have a razor-sharp mind, you can just sit down and say, this is not me, take it away.

"This is one of the most ancient spiritual processes, and there are many step-by-step methods to get there," Sadhguru concluded. "In India, we call this 'nethi-nethi-nethi—this is not it, this is not it, this is not it.' Piece by piece, you take yourself apart. If you are sharp, you can do it this way, but it is better if you use all the dimensions which are you."

When I look back at this time in my life without yoga and meditation, Sadhguru was right. I was all worked up with my own expectations about things. I expected other drivers to drive a certain way. It was just my ego all puffed up big. It didn't even dawn on me that I might feel better if I went back to doing my meditation. I blamed everyone else—the other motorists, my coworkers, and even my wife.

After the incident with the SUV, the traffic was poking along very slowly, so I decided to stop somewhere and wait for it to clear. I went into a restaurant and sat at the bar and ordered a rum and coke, which is something I hadn't done since I started meditation and yoga two years earlier. But, now that I was no longer practicing, a drink sounded pretty good. I drank it down quickly and ordered another one.

Somewhere between the second and third drink, I calmed down and didn't worry about the mess of contradictions that had been dancing around through my mind. The alcohol had dulled the nonsense, as Sadhguru calls it, but only temporarily.

The funk in which I found myself caused me to start retreating from the extracurricular projects like Toastmasters and my homeowners association. I found someone else to lead both groups and almost immediately stopped attending their meetings.

I even found myself neglecting Project Bloom. I didn't attend as many events, and I didn't have as much patience during Project Bloom team meetings. I had been the leader of Project Bloom for two years, and it seemed like a good time to find someone else to take over.

When I think back about this time in my life, at the time I didn't know how unhappy I had become and how simple the solution was. When I had stopped doing my yoga and meditation practice, the stress and anxiety had returned. My overall mood now was so glum that I blamed everything else around me for the problem. I blamed the company, my manager, my coworkers, and even my wife. No one could make me happy.

To complicate things, my push to develop e-learning courses for the rest of the company had caused a rivalry to develop with the IT training department one floor below. Several times when I was about to get a new project, IT training would swoop in and take it from me.

When I decided to host a meeting of all the training managers and developers for the divisions to discuss the capabilities of our online university, IT training insisted they were just about to call the same meeting. It was a bad time for me to realize I was in the middle of a turf war, so very soon I added IT training to my list of "those to blame" for all my problems.

Someone had asked Sadhguru at the business roundtable about competition in business that seemed to describe my relationship with IT training. Sadhguru had said, "Society is in that state right now, that if you survey the challenges of today's world, one can easily come to a dismaying conclusion. There is a great competition. Those who want to compete can compete. If you don't need the race, why don't you come out? Or at least, why can't you slow down the pace? No, you want to race with everybody because you want to be one up on everybody, especially your neighbor. But you do not want to face the difficulties that arise due to this competition. You should understand this very clearly—whatever action you perform in your life, there are consequences to it. There is no such thing as you must perform only this type of action and must not perform another type of action. You can do anything you want. But, you must be in a state to accept the consequences joyously.

"After performing the action," Sadhguru continued, "crying when you have to face the consequences will not do. Do whatever you want in your life, but tomorrow, when you have to face the consequences, you should not cry and complain. If you can accept this joyously, you can do anything. If you don't have the energy to accept the consequence, you don't have to perform that action. It is not needed. Just because somebody else is doing something, you don't have to attempt it or do it. You do not know the kind of energy they have, isn't it? So, the society has become competitive; you are caught in the rat race. You can compete to the extent you want to. But, if you don't have the need for competition, then come, we will teach you meditation; we will set you on the path of meditation—not because you are useless to anything else, only because the need to compete, the need to be in the rat race has dropped."

I must have somehow remembered what Sadhguru had said because I decided not to compete with IT training. I let them host the meeting of all the training managers and developers, and I didn't pursue projects that I knew they would be after.

I had always thought of myself as an optimist, but a wave of pessimism swept over me and carried me out to sea. Everything that went wrong with any of my projects was amplified by this attitude. At the same time, anger was building inside me that caused me to vent by slamming doors and fantasizing about ways to get even with my imaginary enemies.

Sadhguru had said that whatever you focus on, you breed that and make it grow. I was focused on all the negatives in life, and I was breeding a giant crop of negativity that was growing like weeds in an out-of-control garden.

"It is an unfortunate reality in the world today," Sadhguru had said at the business roundtable, "that most people are too focused on the negativity of life. Whatever you pay attention to, that grows and enlarges itself. Even in the press, certain things need to be exposed, but at the same time focusing just on the negative things that are happening in society will only multiply them. It will enter people's minds in such a way, and people will begin to think that this is all that is happening. People lose hope and trust because most human beings on the planet need to be inspired to act in a certain way. So, it is very important that in society there are lots of positive situations which inspire people to act. Right now as a society and as individuals, we are constantly focusing on the negative, which is an immense disservice to humanity.

"One day, a monk went into the forest to do his spiritual practice," Sadhguru said, beginning a story. "He was there for some time, and he happened to come across a fox whose front legs were severed, probably caught in a hunter's trap. It looked like the wound had completely healed a long time ago, but the fox had survived and he was reasonably well-fed. When the monk saw this, he couldn't believe it because nature is not forgiving about such things, and if you become incapable of getting your own food, you are dead in nature. But, this fox could not move anywhere; he just sat under a tree, and he looked reasonably well-fed.

"To the monk's amazement," Sadhguru continued, "that evening he found a lion had come with the carcass of an animal that he had hunted and put whatever leftover meat was there in front of the fox. The fox then ate. The monk couldn't believe his eyes. Every two or three days, the lion came and put some meat in front of the fox, and it went on. So, the monk thought, 'This is a message from God. This is a divine sign. This can't be anything less than this. A lion feeding a fox which is crippled is a miracle.' So, the monk thought, 'This is a message for me. When a crippled fox can get its food to itself wherever it is sitting, why can't I, a monk on the path of the divine, get my food the same way? Why should I go into town to beg for alms? Instead of sitting and meditating, I have been going to the town for food.'

"So, the monk chose a remote part of the forest," Sadhguru said, "behind a rock. He went and meditated for three days, but from the fourth day onward he could not meditate. He only clutched his belly as he sat because hunger overtook him. Eighteen days passed. By then, he was weak and had become very feeble. He was still waiting for a divine act to happen.

"A yogi happened to be passing this way," Sadhguru explained. "He heard the rasping breath of this man; he came looking, and he asked, 'What happened to you? Why are you here like this in this condition?' The monk narrated the fox and the lion story and said, 'You tell me. You are the wise one. Is this not a sign from the divine? Is this not God's message to me?' The yogi looked at him and said, 'Definitely this is God's message. This is definitely a divine sign. But why are you imitating the crippled fox? Why didn't you choose to imitate the generous lion?'"

The moral of this story couldn't have applied more to my situation. I was definitely playing the role of the crippled fox. I had somehow switched roles. When I was doing my yoga and meditating every day, I had easily played the role of the generous lion. That's how Project Bloom had started. It was the soul food for the crippled foxes that filled our offices. Now, I had become one of them, and, like the monk, I was weak and feeble and waiting for divine intervention that seemed as if it would never come.

21

A Transformed Work-Life

The thing that helped to pull me out of my depression and anger was an online course about yoga. Jennifer had been editing videos of Sadhguru's classes, and a programming team in India had put together an online version of Sadhguru's course. Jennifer wanted me to see her video work, so I watched the program one weekend. It was like taking his course all over again.

After completing the online program, I was inspired to start doing yoga and meditation again regularly. Within just a few days, I began to crawl out from under the rock where I had been living. I started to feel I was in control of my life again. I was surprised at how quickly the anger inside of me subsided. Sadhguru had talked about this phenomenon and explained the role yoga and meditation could play.

Sadhguru said, "It doesn't matter how much people preach 'Don't get angry.' When certain situations arise, you will get angry anyway. I want you to understand this. It doesn't matter what kind of human being you become; even if you become a super human being, you will never have absolute control over the external world. Whether it is your business or your family or the world, you will never have total control over the external situation.

"But you can have total control over the internal situation," Sadhguru said. "Emotional states you call as anger—what you call as hate—as lust or as compassion and love, from the lowest to the highest, are certain types of expression of the same energy.

"Unfortunately for most people, their fear, their anger, their hatred are the most intense situations in their lives," Sadhguru explained. "Their love is never so intense. Their peace is never so intense. Their joy is never so intense. But, their negatives are intense. So, they experience power in negative situations.

"But, if you transform your energy in a certain way, it naturally becomes compassion and love—then nobody needs to teach you morality," Sadhguru continued. "And slowly as this process goes further, you will reach the pinnacle of self-awareness and experience unity with all life.

"Suppose you start experiencing yourself as a part of the people around you?" Sadhguru suggested. "After that, no one need teach you to be good and tell you don't harm, and don't kill. Once experientially you are a part of everything, then nobody needs to teach you morality. Then you can do something for the situation, but without anger. What you have to do, you do. But when you do it with anger and hatred, it is of no value—whatever you do.

"The whole process of yoga is based on this," Sadhguru explained. "A day will come when even if you are put into the most extreme situation, your energies will remain very calm. How you respond will depend on the situation you are in, who you are, and what your capabilities are, and what means you have. When you act in unity with all life, you act without identity. Only then you can function out of your intelligence.

"Yoga means to cultivate your energy in such a way," Sadhguru concluded, "that gradually it breaks the physical limitations and elevates you to the highest level of awareness—the flowering of human potential."

Even though I was feeling better about things at work and life in general, and I was less than a year away from qualifying for the company's pension, something told me it was time to move on. When I talked to Jennifer about it, she responded with the same advice she had given me four years earlier, "Quit your job and find something you love."

Leaving your job and becoming self-employed can be a scary proposition. It's something a lot of people talk about, but few people ever really do. I had the benefit of having been self-employed in the past, but it was still a difficult decision. While I tried to calculate how much it would cost to pay for my own health benefits and retirement plan, none of it really made any sense on paper. My logical mind said, "Keep your job and get that pension," but Jennifer's voice kept saying, "Find something you love."

Sadhguru had talked about the role intuition plays in decision making. During the business roundtable he had said, "It has become a fad to people to talk about how they came to a decision intuitively, or how guidance came from somewhere else, from another source. Or they had a gut feeling about something. Most of the gut-feeling decisions are taking people down the gutter. It might have worked for some people. It is just that this has always been the way of people who do not have the necessary grasp over the situation, who cannot think their way out of the situations in which they are. They will try to make a decision by flipping a coin. Right now, what is the best thing to do?

"Suppose you have two options which could be life-making or life-breaking if you make the wrong option. You can't make up your mind; what is the best thing to do? Flip a coin?

"Some time ago, I happened to visit an old friend, who happens to be a homeopathic doctor in India," Sadhguru continued. "He's over seventy years of age. He's been into this for a very long time. When I went to his clinic, I happened to notice that some homeopathic medicine-making company had put up an ad there, a poster, which says that they have a medicine which can cure all kinds of snake bites. Having some knowledge about it, I know that fundamentally there are two kinds of snake venoms. One kind will affect your nervous system; another will affect your cardiovascular system. So in the conversation, I just asked the doctor, 'How is this, that somebody's advertising in your clinic that you have a common solution for both kinds of venoms? How is this possible?' He became very grave, and said, 'See, ninety percent of the snakes in India are nonvenomous, so ninety percent of the time this medicine works.'

"When it comes to making decisions, if you have consciously developed your intuitiveness, that's a different dimension altogether. That means you're consciously creating what you want to create. You're consciously going in the direction in which you want to go; that's what is important. How far you go is not important. That wherever you've gotten, you've gotten there consciously, knowing fully well with your eyes open, you have created this because of you, both internally and externally. Then, if one thing goes wrong, correcting it, or if ten things go wrong, correcting it, or if the whole thing collapses, rebuilding it— everything is in your hands."

Like a lot of people considering a job change, I was worried about money. Could I survive without a steady paycheck? How much business could I get if I were self-employed? How much money did I really need to make?

Sadhguru had addressed this question, saying in essence that it wasn't about how much money you made, but what you did with your life that really counts.

"How much you are worth need not necessarily always be looked at in terms of the money that you're being paid," Sadhguru had explained. "How much you're worth should be assessed in terms of what responsibilities have been given to you. The privilege is not just the money that you get; the privilege is that you've been allowed to be able to create something out of which, naturally, you are expecting some money. But money is only a means for us to have a few things. Those things, yes, are needed; to that extent, money is necessary. But fundamentally, you must always assess yourself in terms of what you are doing, whatever you are being asked to do. What is the level of responsibility that's being offered to you? What is the opportunity for you to create something truly worthwhile, both for yourself and everybody around you? Because any work that you do, any work that you do in the world, is truly worthwhile for you only if you are able to touch people's lives in a deep way.

"Now, if you make a movie, you don't want to make a movie that nobody wants to watch," Sadhguru continued. "You don't want to write a book that nobody wants to read. You don't want to build a house where nobody wants to live. You don't want to produce something where nobody wants to use it. In some way, you want to touch people's lives.

"You will see, if you closely observe your life on the surface, you may be thinking many things," said Sadhguru. "But actually one thing that really means something to you is in terms of activities: the activity that you perform should touch people's lives. Right now, there may be many people who are trying to divide their life into work and family. So work is something that you just do for money, and family is something where you want to touch their lives. Whatever money you earn, and whatever you do, whatever you provide—if you find your wife, your husband, your children, or whoever is there, are not at all touched by what you're doing, then you would see suddenly it would become meaningless for you to have the family. Somewhere, you do something, you want people to be touched by it. This aspect need not remain or restrict itself to family alone. It could extend itself into every area of life, whatever you do. It should touch people's lives; that's all that really matters.

"So how deeply you touch people's lives depends on with how much involvement you do this work," Sadhguru continued. "So if that is there, naturally the way you work will be very different. And according to your capabilities, I think people will pay. Sometimes, maybe you will have to bargain a little bit, but generally I think if people realize the value of what you are to that particular business or company, they will pay.

"Let's say you're heading this corporation. You are not paid anything, but they gave you full responsibility for this whole thing," Sadhguru posited. "If you performed well, and the whole world is watching, tomorrow anybody is willing to grab you for anything."

For the next few days, I worked with a special awareness that any day might be my last. I sat at my desk and looked around carefully examining the smallest detail. I looked out the window and enjoyed the view for what might be the last time. And as I went to meetings and had interactions with people, each one was treated with a bit of reverence, since it might be the last time.

I can't say that I just decided one day that I was going to quit. It just seemed to naturally build up within me, along with a certain kind of calmness and confidence that gave me peace and the knowledge that everything was going to be alright.

At the beginning of my next status meeting with Christi, I pulled a letter from my briefcase.

"I've decided to resign and pursue my own business," I told Christi. "This is my letter of resignation."

"Oh, no. I don't want to take it," Christi said protesting. "You've done so much good work here; everyone is going to be sad to see you go."

As we ended our meeting, I gave Christi a hug and went back to my office. I sent out an email to everyone in HR letting them know that I was leaving and why. Within a few moments, my inbox was filled with shocked responses. People dropped by my office with sad, unhappy, unbelieving looks on their faces.

"Why are you leaving?" they would ask.

"I want to do my own thing again," I replied.

"Why are you leaving?" they would repeat, as if they hadn't heard my answer.

I had given two weeks' notice, so I spent the time working on a transition plan and getting my files organized.

One day as I was creating an enormous pile of paper for the shredder, a small group of employees showed up at my door with a going-away present.

I was touched to see them, and thanked them for stopping by.

"We have something for you," said Melissa, pushing a large, wrapped package into my arms.

"Thank you," I said, looking around at the group. I put the package down on my desk.

"You have to open it now," Melissa ordered.

"Okay," I responded happily, ripping into the package in an exaggerated fashion. When I opened the package, I found a beautiful mantel clock with a pendulum and an engraved brass plate across the base.

Again, there were more heartfelt hugs, and eventually everyone left. When I was alone, I looked at the clock and thought about the irony. They had given me my time back—time to find my own way, and time to bloom.

22

The Ten-Step Commute

After deciding to leave my job, before I decided exactly what I was going to do, I went back and listened to Sadhguru's advice during the business roundtable about transforming your work-life. Here are a few of my favorites:

* Regardless of the weather outside today, you are responsible for the weather inside.
* Work in pursuit of your joy.
* With total involvement, you'll find joy no matter what work you've chosen.
* Do work that is worthwhile to the world, and you will find fulfillment.
* Look for the things most needed in the world, decide which of them you are the most passionate about, and then find a way to get involved.
* Use every situation for your internal growth.
* Loosen people up by allowing them to try out different jobs and responsibilities.
* Anything that is not of any wellbeing to the world will not sell forever.
* Even the simplest things can be done creatively.
* If you do just what it takes to get by, work will be a life-taking experience.

- You can lead only by inspiring people.
- Bring humanity into everything you do.
- Make yourself so precious, both at work and home, that people are willing to make adjustments.
- How much you are worth should be assessed in terms of what responsibilities have been given to you, not necessarily in terms of how much money you are paid.
- Invest a certain amount of time every day in your own wellbeing.
- When you are meditative, you are able to respond to situations rather than react to them.
- Dedicate a certain amount of time to create a culture of peace and happiness with your colleagues.
- Be the manager of your own mind, your body, and your own personality. Only then can you manage other people effortlessly.
- The difficult times are quality control to show you who you really are.
- Be a full-time human being.

Now that I was meditating and doing yoga every day, the clarity that it brought helped me look at the situation and see all the possibilities. I had enough money saved to take my time in making a decision. I knew I wanted to write this book about Sadhguru and the business roundtable, and I had ideas for several other business books. I also enjoyed building training courses, since teaching people new skills felt like a worthwhile pursuit that contributed to everyone's wellbeing.

One interesting thing that fell into my lap involved the newly acquired company that I had helped transition to using our online university. They were using a rapid e-learning development tool that was based on the presentation software, PowerPoint. I had been using PowerPoint to develop slides for instructor-led courses as well as distance learning webinars. I had always had a love-hate relationship with PowerPoint because when it first appeared on the market, many of my video customers began to use it for their corporate presentations instead of videos. Because of PowerPoint, my video business went from producing thirty videos a year to only two or three.

The new rapid e-learning development tool was called Articulate. It allowed you to create a nice-looking interactive Web-based course without any programming skills. The newly acquired company had been using Articulate for a couple of years and had developed five courses using the tool. As part of the acquisition, we were able to purchase Articulate, and I was able to learn and use it to support the existing courses. I then began to use it to produce new courses for our HR department. The first few of these courses had just been completed when I decided to leave.

This new development tool and these new courses gave me an idea. I decided to attend the training summit that the IT training department had organized. This was the meeting that I had originally proposed, but turned over to IT training in the middle of our turf war when they insisted they were just about to call for the same thing.

So, even though I was leaving the company, I went to the meeting and met all of the training managers from the various departments and divisions. I let them know I was leaving, and I talked about developing courses with Articulate.

After the meeting, I received several invitations for meetings to talk about their needs. I ended up meeting with five different training managers, and all of them ended up offering me contract projects. In addition, two of the divisions asked me to help manage the LMS and help roll out corporate online universities.

I was suddenly flooded with business, so there was no longer any doubt that I would be self-employed again and could work from home.

The two hours I had spent commuting to my previous job were now replaced by walking ten steps down into my basement. I had a nice office setup with a U-shaped desk, a fast computer with two monitors, and a nice view of a small lake.

Even though you still answer to your customers when you are self-employed, your work speaks for itself. There's a tremendous freedom in not having a manager, not concerning yourself with office politics, and working when you want to work. I wish everyone had a chance to be self-employed for at least some time in their lives.

One of the things I've learned is the value of customer service when you are self-employed. The success of your business depends on whether your customers are happy with your product or service. When I worked in a corporate environment, I was amazed at how my coworkers treated their customers, even though those customers might be internal departments and other employees. There was hardly any concern about customer service. There was more concern about not overloading yourself. There's no incentive to do anything extra, so few people did.

Sadhguru shared some ideas about customer service during the business roundtable. He had said, "You have never found a mother who is asking, 'How do I really love my child?' The care and concern is natural because she holds the child as a part of herself. She may have to learn what is the best type of diet to give to the child, what is the best school to send the child; all these things she has to learn. But, 'What is the best thing I can do for the child? How much can I do for the child?'—about this she need not learn because it's a natural concern. It is how it should be.

"If you are really caring as to what you produce," Sadhguru said pointedly, "if you are really concerned about the people whom you are offering whatever you are offering, then customer service will be taken care of. Maybe there are things to learn as to how to deliver this to people. That is business-specific. One has to learn in that business how to deliver that particular thing."

Sadhguru then added, "So, in a way, I would say that you must be a mother to the world—if you want to run a business joyfully, benefiting you and everybody. If you are manufacturing something and this is going to service somebody whom you love very much, what kind of product would you give? If you give that kind of product, will I make a profit? Definitely. In the long run, people will buy only that which is reliable. Only that which serves them. Only that which comes from a caring attitude. So what kind of customer service is needed? You must treat your customer as your own child—as your only child. Then things will always work."

When I've talked to other people about working from home and being self-employed, they often worry about having the discipline to get something accomplished. Many people I've talked to who are married to their corporate jobs tell me they are afraid they would end up surfing the net all day.

Sadhguru had talked about the importance of discipline in your life. He had said, "Discipline, the word 'discipline,' unfortunately most of the time is understood as regimenting somebody to do what you will," Sadhguru explained. "If I say, or if you tell somebody, that he needs to be disciplined, he understands that he needs to be punished or he needs to be cut down to size. The word discipline does not mean that. Discipline fundamentally means that one is open to learn; one is open to look. So when you say a certain discipline, you mean a certain aspect of learning. So in that sense, discipline is needed so that everybody is in a process of constantly learning. So, if that sense of discipline has to come, we have to bring a huge sense of involvement into the activity that they are performing. If that sense of involvement is not there, one does not learn; one just works to the extent it is necessary. So when you bring a huge sense of involvement, you will see every day they keep coming back with new ideas of what they have picked up in the same work that they have been doing.

"I've personally been constantly encouraging people to look deeper into the nature of activity that they are performing," Sadhguru explained. "It's quite amazing how many times so many small things that we have missed come back to you after so many years of doing the same activity. You think you have looked at it with a fine comb on everything, but somebody comes up with a simple point after many years of performing that activity. Something as simple as cleaning this room, somebody comes out with a revolutionary idea after how many years of cleaning we have done!"

Sadhguru laughed and added, "So every day, if you listen to one hundred things that people have to say, maybe in a year's time you'll get good things to pick up. But you're listening. You're constantly willing to listen to everybody's thing. Or, if you yourself are not able to listen in terms of time, you set up mechanisms where somebody else listens, and they distill it and pass it on to you. These mechanisms I feel are there in every situation, but, most of the time, they will not be consciously set up, nor do a lot of people understand the significance of why these things are there. You want to know everything that's happening because you are constantly seeing how to make things happen better.

"So you have to instill that confidence in people that they can speak," Sadhguru insisted. "It's not wrong to speak about anything that you are doing, or somebody else is doing, how it could be done better. So, if that level of openness is created, bringing discipline will not be an external issue. It is something that everybody is striving for. If just one person has to bring discipline to everybody, then usually it leads back to tyranny. When everybody is striving to see how to make this happen, then there is a discipline without a word being uttered about it.

"So, bringing that sense of involvement in people is the best way to discipline the group," Sadhguru reiterated. "Without their involvement, if you try to discipline them, they'll find a million ways to break it. People are very innovative when it comes to breaking rules."

Sadhguru laughed again and then said, "They'll find a million different ways as to how to break the rule. So you have to be making the right kinds of noises, the kind of noises that people will understand, to show them that your involvement toward them is absolute. So that they also show that involvement in the work they are doing.

"If two people have to work together, working together does not mean you are getting married to them," Sadhguru explained. "But working together is many times more than marriage because you are constantly together. Probably you spend more time with people whom you work than people whom you're married to in many ways."

In my case, I was going to be working again with my wife, Jennifer. Many people had told me that they could never do that. They couldn't imagine spending all day working with their spouse. "We'd tear each other apart," they would say. That sounded more like two tigers stuck together in a cage than two people who were sharing their lives together, but there was no point in arguing. Jennifer and I had developed our relationship to the point where we could work together, eat together, play together, and meditate together. In other words, live together twenty-four hours a day.

Sadhguru had ended his discussion of discipline with a story about a hyena, a monkey, and a lion. "It happened like this," Sadhguru began. "One day a hyena came and complained to his friend, who was a monkey, that every time he passes through a certain pathway, a lion always bothers him. He comes and mauls him. So, the monkey said, 'Today let's go together. If he bothers you, I will come and help you.' So both were walking together, and the lion came out of his den and went after the hyena as usual. And the monkey ran up the tree and sat there. This particular day, the lion really gave the hyena the mauling of his life. And the monkey just sat up there, and then somehow the hyena escaped and went away. Then they again met. The hyena said, 'What did you do? You said you will help me. You just sat up on the tree and watched.' The monkey said, 'You were laughing so much, I thought you were winning!'"

Everyone around the business roundtable laughed at Sadhguru's story. He then added one more piece of wisdom. "So you must make the right kind of noises; otherwise, people misunderstand," Sadhguru chuckled. "Your intentions may be okay, but still you have to make the right kind of noises. So if you want to bring some discipline into the team—even if your intentions are good, it may be for his wellbeing—but unless you make the right kind of noises, it doesn't go across."

Sadhguru gave me a completely different way to think about discipline and how it relates to being self-employed. If you think about it as being open to learn and open to look, then having discipline is the perfect formula for success. You have to be adaptable, reinvent yourself from time to time, and try to stay up to date on the latest business trends.

It took some time to make the transition from corporate life, and a few late nights to catch up on some deadlines, but soon I had a daily routine down to the point that I was at least 50 percent more productive than in my previous corporate life. And, the time saved from not having to commute was an added bonus.

In addition, Jennifer and I could now multiply our efforts as a team on the same projects. Our combination of skills made us a self-contained e-learning development company without the need for any other outside assistance.

Working out of our basement with no office rent, we hardly had any overhead other than Internet access and the occasional printer ink cartridge.

It may sound like a fairy tale, but within a few months we had projects from corporate security, finance, marketing, and HR.

In addition, several people whom I had hired as contractors at various times in my previous job had moved onto jobs at other companies. When they heard that I had started my own e-learning development business, they hired us to help them. At one point, we were working for five different companies at the same time.

As the year came to an end and I took the time to examine my finances, I realized that I had earned over four times what I would have earned if I had kept my corporate job. It was like working dog-years. Each self-employed year was like working four corporate years.

I remembered that Sadhguru had offered advice about business profitability and what businesses must do to stay profitable.

"When you set up a business, naturally because you are investing a certain amount of money, the first interest of any business will be to make a profit," Sadhguru began. "But over a period of time, when the business grows, you begin to understand that profitability is not a separate issue from the rest of the life that's happening around you. Profitability need not just mean getting this much money in this much time. Profitability means that you have insured a long-term wellbeing of the institution that you have set up.

"You see every year hundreds of companies are folding because people are not thinking long-term wellbeing," Sadhguru explained. "Long-term wellbeing, not just in terms of your life—if you value the institution you have set up, if you value what this institution has to offer to the world—then you would want this to exist even beyond you.

"So, profitability just does not mean this year's balance sheet," Sadhguru reiterated. "Profitability means that you are insuring solid foundations for the company to grow and prosper on a long-term basis. On a long-term basis, if any company has to live and prosper, then they have to be concerned about everything in the world around them. Otherwise, they will not survive long term. Only those companies which invested on long-term R&D and things like that have survived for a long time. Others are like a flash in the pan; they happen today and tomorrow they go.

"If you build the right kind of people, those people will in turn build the right kind of company," said Sadhguru. "Because no matter what corporation you talk about, what type of human beings are in key places in that corporation decide how far the corporation goes, isn't it? How smoothly they function in those areas where they need to function, is what decides how far it goes. So, if you are concerned about your profitability on a long-term basis, you must be concerned about the people whom you are working with, those who are working for you, and those whom you service.

"What kind of product you put to the people, are they happy with it, or is it for their wellbeing?" Sadhguru asked. "Today there are products where for the last three generations people have been using the same product. They don't need any marketing because 'my grandmother told me you must drink this. She made sure I drank only that. And my mother told me the same thing. Now I will tell the same thing to my child.' So this is long term. There are many companies like this, which have survived without any great bombastic marketing, but from generation to generation people are still using the same product because they have been concerned about the wellbeing of the person who uses the product. As long as we are truly looking at the wellbeing of the people who work for us, and the people who are being serviced by us, and people who buy the product that we produce, then the long-term profitability and wellbeing of the corporation is definitely taken care of."

Sadhguru continued, "So what money you make is not the thing. How you are growing, how happy people are who are working for you, and how happy people are who are being serviced by you is the important thing for the health of the corporation. Without that, a corporation cannot be healthy. People who are working for you should be happy. People who are buying your products should be happy. Only then the corporation is healthy. I think that's what everybody should be concerned about. Profitability will anyway happen."

For our little two-person business, Jennifer and I were enjoying our work, and we were producing a high-quality product for people who seemed to appreciate the quality. Because of that, we didn't do any marketing. We obtained new business through word of mouth, as one happy customer told another.

As Sadhguru had said, if you do something that contributes to the wellbeing of others, then you've added value that justifies the time you spend on this earth.

23

Blooming Today

Just before leaving my corporate job where I helped start Project Bloom, I stepped down as the team leader and found two team members to take over as coleaders. To encourage them to accept the position, I gave the position a title: "Landscape Architect."

After the leadership transition, I attended Project Bloom team meetings up until my resignation from the company. I did my best to contribute without butting it or pushing my opinion on the new leaders. They took turns running meetings, which helped balance the workload.

I'm happy to say that Project Bloom continued to flourish. I've kept in contact with one of the Bloom leaders over the past few years to see how things were going. There have been changes, and I think most of them have been good. For example, after I left, there was less focus on employee recreational activities like monthly games, crafts, and restaurant outings, and more focus on employee development through lunch-and-learns and volunteer projects. In fact, volunteering has become one of the biggest aspects of the program. The VP who originally approved Project Bloom and suggested that we award points for giving blood decided to offer a new policy where employees could take off time from work each month to volunteer somewhere in the community. These volunteer projects are now coordinated through what used to be Project Bloom.

To keep the program on track, one of the directors was assigned to the team to help run meetings and to coordinate all of the activities. This has helped the program encourage more involvement from management in all of the activities that are offered. The program is now more integrated with the strategic development plans for the department and the company.

This latest version of Project Bloom is probably the best model for sharing with other organizations. Having direct management involvement in running the program and aligning the activities with strategic development plans is a win-win scenario that makes a program like Project Bloom a much easier sell.

One thing I regret about my involvement with Project Bloom is that I wasn't able to include meditation as part of the program. At the time, we didn't have Isha Kriya available, which is currently used in many corporate settings across the country. If I were starting a program like Project Bloom today, I would definitely incorporate the Isha Kriya meditation because meditation has so many physical and psychological benefits.

I have seen more and more signs that meditation is becoming a more accepted mainstream practice in US organizations. Recently, I read about a program that is teaching meditation to returning veterans from Iraq and Afghanistan. Meditation is being offered to them as a treatment for PTSD.

I saw an article in *Fortune* magazine that listed a number of corporate leaders who say meditation played a major role in their success. From the CEO of Medtronic, to an NBA coach and the CEO of Salesforce.com, all say that meditation has improved their ability to think creatively.

Following up on Sadhguru's visit to Google, I discovered that Google has organized twice-weekly open meditation hours during business hours. They've also hosted Tibetan monks who have visited with employees and taught meditation.

A recent study by the University of Wisconsin involved experiments using cranial electrodes and MRI scans to study the effects of meditation on people. The basic finding from the study was that the brain functioning of serious meditators was profoundly different from that of non-meditators in ways that suggest an elevated capacity to concentrate and to manage emotions.

Findings from the National Institutes of Health, the University of Massachusetts, and Mind/Body Medical Institute at Harvard University reveal that meditation enhances the qualities companies need most from knowledge workers: increased brain-wave activity, enhanced intuition, better concentration, and the alleviation of common aches and pains.

Increasingly, companies are finding that meditation classes fit nicely with their health and wellness programs. In addition to Google, companies like Apple, Yahoo!, Deutsche Bank, AOL Time Warner, AstraZeneca Pharmaceuticals, and Hughes Aircraft are offering regular meditation classes.

On one of Sadhguru's visits to the United States, he taught meditation classes at General Motors, Pontiac, and Chrysler.

Meditation programs are even being tried in prisons. Sadhguru has taught several prison yoga and meditation programs for inmates who have been sentenced to life-in-prison. The warden at one prison reported that normally he was forced to send thirty prisoners a month to the isolation cell as punishment for rules violations. A month after taking Sadhguru's yoga and meditation class, not one inmate had to go to the isolation cell. Today in southern India, Isha Yoga is required for prisoners.

If you are interested in learning to meditate, or are interested in a corporate meditation program, check out some of the websites that are listed in the appendix of this book.

If you are interested in organizing a program like Project Bloom in your company, check out the Project Bloom website that is also listed in the appendix. There, you'll find articles about the program as well as stories about the impact of meditation on businesses. A Project Bloom manual is also available if you would like a copy. If you do set up your own program like Project Bloom, send an email and let me know how it's going. And, if you end up creating a book club like we did, I've got a great suggestion for your group's first book.

24

Corporate Consciousness

Approximately eighteen months after Sadhguru conducted the business roundtable, he returned to personally conduct another yoga and meditation class. While he was in town, Jennifer and I were asked to come to his temporary corporate apartment and shoot another interview about business topics. Sadhguru had been invited to speak at the World Economic Forum in Davos, Switzerland, on the subject of "Inclusive Economics."

It was a different apartment complex than the one where I had picked up Sadhguru before. Leela, Sadhguru's assistant, greeted us at the door and welcomed us inside. She showed us the living room, and we began making plans for how we would set up the room for the shoot.

As we were setting up, a few more local meditators arrived to help. With the extra assistance, we had all of the lights and camera gear set up within about thirty minutes.

As we finished, Sadhguru came out of his bedroom and greeted us. He wasn't wearing his normal turban and shawl. Instead, he was bareheaded and wearing a comfortable oversized sweatshirt, like anyone might wear when relaxing around the house. I was surprised when he nodded in my direction and said, "How are you doing, Kevin?"

"I'm fine. How are you?"

"Busy. Lots going on back in India." He then made it a point to greet Jennifer and the rest of the volunteers.

Leela had made some food, and Sadhguru had something to eat as he talked informally us. There was a question on my mind regarding why he was speaking at the World Economic Forum. While it was a prestigious event, I wondered why he was going and how that audience would react to a yogi from India. So, when there was a short break in the conversation, I jumped in.

"Sadhguru," I began, "I'm wondering about the World Economic Forum and whether anything you say will change their attitudes. Isn't it just a bunch of business and political leaders who are looking for ways to increase their wealth?"

"What we need in the world is not just wealth creation," Sadhguru said. "We need to create wellbeing. Wealth is just one of the tools toward human wellbeing, not the whole of it. But right now, people are pursuing it like a religion. We have turned money into God, and we are pursuing it relentlessly. Money is just a means; it is not an end by itself. We created it for our convenience, but in pursuit of wealth creation, we are destroying the very planet on which we live."

Sadhguru finished eating and stopped for a moment to wipe his mouth. He then continued, "Whether you make a safety pin or build a computer or a car or some great machine, whatever you do, you are digging it out of the planet. We must decide how much to dig. We must also think of how much Mother Earth can take. If we are not responsible about this, we may completely destroy the planet with our ideas of wealth creation, which we are doing today in many ways. Instead of thinking of wealth creation, if we think of creating human wellbeing, we would just do whatever is needed and to the extent it is needed."

Sadhguru paused for a moment and ate. It gave me a chance to make a comment. "Telling people to stop creating wealth is going to be a hard sell," I said. "I don't know how the World Economic Forum will take it, but creating wealth is all we think about in the United States."

"We must first understand what our idea of wealth is," Sadhguru responded. "Is it just about more buildings, more machines, more cars—more of everything? More and more is death, isn't it? In the most affluent societies in the world—for example, in the United States of America, forty-three percent of the population is on antidepressants on a regular basis. If you just withdraw one particular medication from the market, almost half the nation will go crazy. That is not wellbeing.

"Generally, an American citizen has everything anybody would dream of," Sadhguru continued. "There is wealth, but no wellbeing. What are you going to do with this wealth? When I go to the West and ask, 'Why don't you meditate?' the common statement everywhere is 'Oh, but we've got bills to pay.' I said, 'Why do you guys generate so many bills?' If your whole life is about paying bills, why generate those damn bills? You can curtail yourself and live more comfortably, isn't it? To pay all those bills you are just working endlessly. What is the point? The whole society is doing it. It doesn't matter; they are driven by somebody else.

"If you have any sense, you must drive yourself to the extent that you are comfortable," Sadhguru said. "There may be somebody who can do a thousand things in a day without suffering or being stressed. Maybe you can do only three things in a day; it's okay. You don't try to do what somebody else does. This is the biggest problem; we are trying to do things like somebody else.

"When it comes to outside situations," Sadhguru continued, "no two human beings have come with the same level of capability. Your neighbor may have a one hundred-bedroom house. Maybe he likes to live in a hotel. For yourself, you must decide how much; you don't do things like him. Trying to do things like somebody else is the wrong way to approach life. We need to decide how much of what we should do in our lives—how much outside activity or inner wellbeing or social wellbeing would keep our life balanced without ruining us and the atmosphere around us.

"But unfortunately, that intelligence is missing," Sadhguru said, shaking his head. "It is insane the way we are going because that kind of lifestyle is just not sustainable. It can only crash, and we will have to learn the lesson the hard way.

"Today, we are almost seven billion people," Sadhguru said. "This is the largest human population ever, and in nurturing this kind of population, so many other species on the planet have become extinct. The projected population in 2050 is nine and a half billion people. Can you imagine the world with nine and a half billion people in just another four decades?

"Either we correct this ourselves or nature will do the correction," Sadhguru warned. "If nature does the correction, it is going to be very cruel. The choice that we have is to either live sensibly or senselessly. The choice is not about wealth and poverty. The choice is between expressing our needs and finding fulfillment in a sensible way or in a blatant manner."

We were all quiet after his ominous warning. I had not realized there were already seven billion people on the planet. I then thought about all the senseless ways we were destroying ourselves under the guise of convenience: single serving packages, bottled water, and all of the many ways we've misused energy like gasoline, electricity, coal, and natural gas. Having an enlightened yogi speak to these leaders at the World Economic Forum might help open the world's eyes, so I understood why he was going and why he wanted to speak.

After he finished eating, Sadhguru went back to his room and changed clothes, returning a short time later wearing his familiar tan turban with a beautiful multicolored shawl.

Once he was in place in front of the camera, I made some final adjustments to the lights. Jennifer started recording, and Sadhguru began speaking.

"A whirlwind of economic activity is happening in the world, especially in India today," Sadhguru said with outstretched arms. "Our economy is growing like never before. Everything is bursting at the seams; just holding it in place has been a huge circus for everybody involved. This could either bring a lot of wellbeing, or lead to total destruction.

"Of four major forces in the world—politics, military, religion, and economics—that decide the quality of people's lives to a large extent, the economic force seems to be the one capable of bringing about some unification and sensible action. The other forces are merely dictated by belief. People of two different religions or politicians of two different ideologies can never come to an agreement. Only a businessman will be willing to make a deal—even with the devil if it is a good deal.

"Today's corporations have grown to such size that they are as big as governments. Their goal is no longer just profit, but expansion. That is why today's corporate leader is required to travel extensively, handle a variety of issues and complexities and, above all, deal with people from diverse backgrounds and cultures. Therefore, a truly successful corporate leader should be versatile and able to multitask in complex situations. If any human being has to handle very complex issues on a daily basis, it is very important that he is spiritually equipped.

"What we refer to as spirituality," Sadhguru explained, "is the technology for inner wellbeing. Unfortunately, in the course of transferring spiritual processes through generations, cultural and religious influences became part of it. A spiritual process that is free of cultural and religious trappings is most needed today. It need not be taught as a philosophy or a belief system. It can be imparted as simple methods that would naturally lead to a more inclusive way of experiencing life.

"It is important for the corporations to cultivate a favorable atmosphere for this," Sadhguru continued. "Meditation spaces in corporate centers will bring a great sense of harmony and wellbeing in individuals and the organization. This will pay off in a big way.

"The people who make decisions for everybody," Sadhguru said, "should be in a good condition because their decisions affect many. I want to shift the business community from operating for limited ambitions to a larger vision. I want to see them more joyful because joyful people are more generous, more sensible, more flexible, and always more life-oriented. It is very important that they are more peaceful and joyful from within, and not because of the quarterly balance sheet.

"If that does not happen," he continued, "the economic forces can be deadly dangerous. Right now, we have made economics the most important aspect of our lives. When the economic engine drives everything, then naturally we become very gross, because it is all about pulling and pushing and somehow being on top. There is no room for any subtleness, gentleness, or concern when competition rules.

"In the past, overambitious and ruthless people led the economy," Sadhguru explained. "But now there are many truly sensitive and wonderful human beings on top. But even they are thinking in terms of 'goodness' or, in other words, they want to make a lot of money and do a little bit of charity. But, charity is neither sustainable, nor a solution.

"The economic engine runs only if people keep buying and buying," Sadhguru warned. "So we try to include more and more people into our list of clients or customers. The idea is to include the whole seven billion people on the planet.

"Right now, only about forty percent of the world's population is involved in economic activities in a meaningful way," Sadhguru insisted. "If you exclude the other sixty percent of the population, neither your market base nor your human resources expand. Expansion is inclusion. You can expand either by conquering or by including. Conquering is a violent way of doing things. So we need to have a model where all businesses can work with more inclusion. That is why we are talking about inclusive economics. It is a gentler way of doing business."

Sadhguru added, "When I was invited to attend a business forum for the first time, a particularly belligerent CEO came up to me and asked, 'What are you doing here?' I knew that he would not understand anything except his own jargon, so I said, 'All I am doing here is expanding my market base.'

"If we want a gentler and more compassionate economic process," Sadhguru offered, "it is not charity, but inclusiveness that is needed. If there is no sense of inclusiveness in individual human beings, the systems they create or actions they perform will never lead to inclusiveness. Individuals who do not experience this inclusiveness end up creating very exclusive processes. Spirituality is about living here in an all-inclusive way, experiencing everything as a part of yourself. One basic aspect of the spiritual process is that it makes one an all-inclusive human being. At the same time, it will hugely equip the individual to be more efficient, more capable, more balanced, and more productive. This is good for business. This is good for the world."

As Sadhguru was talking, for some reason I drifted off into a daydream as I'm prone to do. I was thinking about a presentation I had made to the VP of public relations at the company where I worked. I had an idea for a volunteer project for Project Bloom that would involve retirees from the company offering coaching and mentoring services to high school students. The project would require a budget, so I had been advised by Mike, my manager, to talk to the VP of PR. I had sent her an email along with an attached proposal, and she had invited me for a meeting. During that meeting, she told me that while my idea was a good one, it wasn't right for the company. They had to target their giving in directions that not only benefited the community, but also benefited the company. As an example, the company owned cable TV systems, so one of their acts of charity was to give money to the Boys & Girls Club to create an educational program that taught disadvantaged kids the technology of cable television. The kids that graduated from the program would be qualified for jobs as cable TV installers.

When the VP explained this to me, it made sense. And it tied back to what Sadhguru was saying. Corporations could do more to include those who had previously been excluded, and it could be done in a way that was beneficial to the company and the community. This cable TV program was the perfect example.

I was so deep in the middle of my daydream that I didn't notice Sadhguru had finished his presentation. Looking right at me, he seemed to sense something. He then suddenly said, "Kevin, what do you think?"

I felt like a kid in school who's not been paying attention, and who was just called upon by the teacher to perform some complicated math problem on the chalkboard. Not really knowing what I should say, I opened my mouth and words started coming out.

"I was just thinking about a program we started in the business where I work," I said, as the thoughts in my head formed into words on my lips. "It was based on that business roundtable discussion we had a year or so ago. I took some of your advice, and we created a program designed to recognize, appreciate, and develop the employees. We called it Project Bloom. It has been very successful. The morale of the employees has changed. And many of my coworkers have really bloomed. They are doing things no one would have thought possible a year ago. We're doing a lot of corporate volunteer work. We're going out as a group and working on community projects together."

Sadhguru looked at me and smiled. "Human lives become beautiful because we put our heart into what we're doing. It doesn't matter what we're doing. Whether we are sweeping the floor, or managing the country, or whatever we are doing, if we put our heart into what we are doing, it is beautiful to be doing that activity. So, I hope everybody here is putting their hearts into what they're doing, and living in an atmosphere where people are passionate about what they're doing."

"That's not the situation at the place where I work," said a voice to my left. It was Jim, a meditator who had come to help us set up. He continued, somewhat disgusted. "Morale is terrible there. The managers manipulate, threaten, and coerce the employees, and I feel stuck. I'm really miserable there."

"Once you step into the world, there's going to be a lot of filth," Sadhguru said, shaking his head. "There is corruption, there is nonsense, there are so many things happening everywhere. There are some set of people, a certain set of people, who will develop an allergy for this filth. They can't stand it. They usually run to the Himalayas for they are allergic to filth; they can't take it. They want everything pure. But such a thing will not happen, because the filth of the world has entered our minds. Whether we empower that filth or not, is all the option that we have. But we cannot avoid the filth; it is there.

"Another set of people, a large segment of people unfortunately have merged into the filth," Sadhguru continued. "What we call as filth can also become great manure. A lotus flower has always been the main symbolism for Indian spirituality. A lotus flower grows best where the filth is thick. This filth, which is stinking so much you can't bear it, has transformed itself into a fragrant beautiful flower."

Sadhguru picked up a flower that was resting in a vase on the small table beside him. He twirled the stem in his hand, and then smelled the fragrant bud.

"This option also is with us every moment of our lives," he said, looking at the flower. "If the atmospheres that we live in make us, we cannot call ourselves managers. If we make the atmospheres that we live in, only then we can call ourselves managers."

I thought about Sadhguru's response to Jim. He was giving Jim the same advice he had given me during the business roundtable: don't let the external influences determine who you are. Change yourself, and then do what you can to change the culture of your business. I also thought it was symbolic that Sadhguru was saying this while smelling a flower.

Sadhguru put the bloom down and looked out at the rest of us in the room. "Being a manager means that we are going to create whatever we see as the most beautiful thing to happen right now. Allowing situations to create you is not management at all. Creating the situations that you want is management.

"Let's say somebody got a job," Sadhguru explained, "and the first day they went and sat behind this desk. This desk was the most fantastic place in the world. But within a few years, behind the same table, they're manufacturing high blood pressure, diabetes, and ulcers. This is not because there is something wrong with the jobs that we do. This is not because there is something wrong with the world that we live in. It is simply because we have not paid sufficient attention to ourselves. We have paid too much attention to what is outside.

"Making yourself capable," he continued, "not only in terms of management skills and other things, but also making yourself capable as a human being, to go through situations untouched, is to be like that lotus flower. Even if you're in the filthiest of situations, to maintain your beauty and fragrance, if one has this, he will float through this life untouched. If one doesn't have it, life will eat him up in so many ways.

"It is my wish and my blessing," Sadhguru offered, "that you will manage your businesses in a much better way than the previous generations of people have done.

"Right now, the Isha Foundation is run by young people," Sadhguru explained. "We have hundreds of centers around India and outside the country. Everything is managed by very young people. People who have been with us for fourteen, fifteen years, they're just in their early thirties now. Very young people. No senior people, no experienced people, just young people, raw hands. I took this as a challenge to make it happen through them, not using any kind of experience. I'm not against experience, but I wanted to make a statement that incredible things can be done, not because we know how to do it, but because we're committed that we want it to happen, that's all."

Sadhguru added, "Today, this has grown into an organization with over two hundred and fifty thousand active volunteers around the world. And we have taken on enormous projects of social significance. All those things are handled by volunteers who are not paid for it. They spend from their own pockets and do great things. And you need to understand that managing these people, managing volunteers, is much more difficult than managing paid employees because you can't fire them for inefficiency or indiscipline or whatever, because they're there on a voluntary basis.

"So, the people who manage these volunteer situations, very young people, without any qualifications, they're such fantastic managers of people," Sadhguru said emphatically. "The way they manage the situations, the way they conduct thousands of people has such an exemplary example in the community there.

"Fundamentally, management is your ability to be capable of inspiring people to do their best," Sadhguru said. "And that's all we can do. If everybody around us is doing their best, that's the best possible management that can happen. So this is not going to come with manipulation. This is only going to come with dedication; this is only going to come with love; this is only going to come because you are willing to give yourself one hundred percent to the person who is sitting next to you at that moment.

"Oh, is all this possible?" Sadhguru asked. "Is it not all utopian? You think this is not possible in the corporate sector? I am telling you, we are working in the prisons; we are working in the rural areas; we are working in major corporations in the world; it doesn't matter what kind of person you meet. If you just learn to touch the core of this humanity, then you see, every human being is willing to do his best for you, always.

"If you do not create the people who truly love us and want to do their best," Sadhguru reiterated, "then management is going to be a pain; management is going to be a huge suffering. Only when people around us really want to do their best for you, only then management can happen wonderfully.

"Our lives become beautiful not because of what we do," Sadhguru concluded. "Our lives become beautiful simply because we have included everybody around us as a part of our dream of wellbeing."

25

Creating Your Life

For most of my life, I've wanted to be a writer. When I was sixteen, I wrote a massive three hundred-page story titled, "All in a Daze Work." It was a surrealistic story about a group of people who lived inside large pipes that were part of an abandoned sewer construction project. The pipes had been lined up along the road, and people had moved into them and made them their homes. They had chairs, tables, and lamps. They watched TV, read the paper, and brushed their teeth inside these compact, round apartments. In the story, one guy had a vision that you didn't have to live in these sewer pipes, and that instead it was possible to live inside square or rectangular houses. Everyone laughed at him and eventually ran him out of sewer pipe land. At first he was sad and worried, but eventually he escaped the boundaries of the construction project and found beautiful landscaped neighborhoods nearby with roomy two-story houses. And there were wonderful people there, living wonderful lives, and of course he lived there happily ever after.

That story was pounded out on an old manual Royal typewriter, and the only copy is stored away in a dusty box in my garage. Now that I look back and think about it, it's a great analogy for the way things typically are in business today compared to the way things could be. All you need is a vision in order to create life and work the way you want it to be. One of the reasons for writing this book was to share the idea for Project Bloom, so that even if you find yourself living and working in sewer pipe land, you'll know there is something else better out there.

Project Bloom

Not only is this transformation possible for you personally, it is also possible for your workplace. I believe that meditation puts you into direct contact with your true self. It is the "you" that was there just after you were born, before you were given a name. It looked out from your eyes and saw the world without labels and without judgment. That's your true self, and when you are able to communicate with it directly, and tell it what you want to create, it is like a genie in a bottle: your wish is its command. One of the ways I've transformed my life is by turning myself into the writer I always dreamed of being.

Meditation really does work to put you in control of your life, so that you can create the kind of life you want. As my friend Michael had said, "It is literally the single most important thing a person can learn in their lifetime." I agree 100 percent.

Several of my friends and colleagues noticed the changes in me and asked what I was doing. When I told them, they eventually took Sadhguru's classes and learned to meditate.

One of my colleagues was Jackie, the HR director of talent development. Her job involved maximizing employees' strengths and keeping them engaged.

"You brought calmness to things," Jackie told me. "When things were getting hectic, I saw how calm you were. I needed something like that, so I was interested in finding out how you did it."

Since learning to meditate, Jackie has changed jobs twice, her last job being a jump to running her own business. "People sometimes feel trapped by their jobs," Jackie told me. "They call it the golden handcuffs syndrome. Those handcuffs keep people from exploring other interests. I'm not letting anyone keep me long enough that I end up having to do things that I regret later. I don't have fifteen to twenty years logged with a company, so I don't have lots to lose when I feel like I want to leave and try something else."

When Jackie's last company announced that there were going to be layoffs, Jackie's manager commented, "You are the only one out of twenty that I have to lay off who seems happy about it." The reason was that Jackie was in control. She had a plan. In fact, she came up with three plans. Eventually, she was offered a severance package that gave her time to start her own consulting business. Within three months after leaving, she had her first customer and project.

"Have there been any benefits during this transition that came from your meditation practice?" I asked.

"When I get under stress, I start looking for solutions," Jackie replied. "Meditation gave me great clarity and the calmness to detach. Before, my emotions had been dominant, and I could not think logically. Now, I calm myself and I begin to think. It gave me a perspective that 'this is today' rather than getting all worked up about the past or the future.

"When I returned from my first meditation class, my manager could tell something had changed in me," Jackie continued. "Several people noticed and commented. 'You are in a completely different place,' they told me. The business couldn't touch me anymore emotionally. You can't hurt me. I'm not taking these things personally. I ended up responding to my manager in a more kind way, and it brought back more kindness in return.

"Many of the other people I work with are overly logical," Jackie explained. "On the other hand, I was overly emotional. I was feeling things to the point that I couldn't think clearly. For those who are overly logical, the meditation helps them balance so they can relate to people and situations better. For me, it was just the opposite. The meditation helped me balance out my emotions, so I could logically work things out."

When the layoffs came at Jackie's previous company, her colleagues could see that she was responding rather than reacting to the situation. They came to her for advice, and she coached them.

"I helped them make plans just as I had," Jackie explained. "The company could make its own choice, but I had a choice on how to respond. I could pick from three possible plans I created. So many other people were just waiting until the company told them its decision, and then they were going to come up with a plan. In my case, all of my plans were going to take me on a path where I would have an engaging environment and where I could make a difference."

When I asked Jackie for something specific that changed within her, she explained it in this way: "I usually go and collect a lot of opinions, and then I sort through them. The meditation has given me the clarity to sort through them much quicker. I quickly saw that these seven were not the ones, and these three were strong possibilities. In the past before meditating, if I had ten things to think about, I would think about all ten with equal importance. I would overthink and overanalyze things. But, now it is different. That's what I mean about clarity from the meditation. These were the three options that would give me the life I wanted.

"If you don't have a mind-set that you can grow, you feel limited and stagnant," Jackie added. "If you say, 'I love horses, but I'm clumsy and can't ride them,' then you limit yourself and you'll never try. But, if you say, 'I love horses; I'm kind of clumsy, but I can get better,' then you open up the possibilities. There is something in meditation that opens up those possibilities. It changes your mind-set."

Project Bloom

Another friend of mine, Leslie, who is a leadership consultant in HR, shared another example of how meditation helps you create the kind of life you want. She and her husband, Carl, decided to move from their long-time home to be closer to Leslie's father who lived in another state. This meant not only selling their home, but also finding new jobs. Plus, they chose to make this move in the middle of an economic recession.

I asked Leslie how being a meditator affected their decisions.

"The amount of work that has to happen for something like this is astronomical," Leslie said. "But it just happened easily. Everything that I needed just fell into place. If we hit a bump in the road, it never really felt like a bump. I was always just looking at reality and saying, 'Oh, what do we do now?' I never thought, 'Oh my God, that's so stressful.' Or, 'That is a huge barrier.' It was more like, 'This is interesting. What do we need to do?' It was like that continuously.

"We were up north in Detroit where the market is so bad," Leslie continued. "And everybody was saying, 'You can't find a new job. The economy is bad. You can't find a new home; you can't sell the one you've got.' Those were the overriding messages from my company and in the newspaper. We had to push past the negative messages that were saying this is not the time to be changing jobs or trying to sell a house; these things can't happen. I might not have tried this if I were not meditating. Meditation just sort of rooted me internally, so I'm not paying as much attention to the negative messages. I'm paying a lot more attention to what I want to do, what I want to create in my life, and what I need to do to create it, regardless of what anybody else says. That's the biggest change that comes from doing meditation daily. That's the clarity that everyone talks about, inner clarity. So, when the insanity is going on around you, the negative messages are going on around me, I seem to be able to stay focused on what I want to create. And of course, your behavior is in line with that. Your external actions are in line with that. Because your mind is clear on what it wants. I think that is the magic that is behind meditation."

Leslie told me that she and Carl sold two homes in less than a year in Detroit. Carl then pinpointed ten companies where he would like to work. He went around and talked to people, he got new contacts from the people with whom he talked, and he ended up getting a job offer. He then found a neighborhood he liked, a house he liked, and picked out a school his daughter would like. So, he made the decision, took the job, and a short time later, not even a month after, one of the companies where he really wanted to work had an opening and offered him a position. So, Carl changed jobs one more time and took the job he had really targeted all along. He ended up getting what he wanted because the focus was there. He was willing to take the risk.

"It's like when you are a monkey between two trees," Leslie explained. "You have to let go of one tree in order to leap out and grab the other. That's why meditation is so important when you are taking these risks. You need the clarity it brings to not get distracted when jumping from tree to tree like that, to stay focused on the tree that you want to jump to, and not to second-guess your decision midway through the air. It strengthens you to make these leaps. You grow tremendously, and the things you want, they manifest."

In addition to Carl's job change, Leslie had to make a career change herself. She resigned from her job in the training department of a health care company, but after resigning, several people encouraged her to continue working for the company as a remote consultant.

"I work for a pretty conservative company," Leslie told me. "Work from home is not common at all. So, I resigned, but then the paradigm shifted for me. I was thinking I was leaving, and I would look for something in my new town, but then I thought perhaps there might be another way. So, I talked to my manager and she said, 'Yes, there could be another way.'"

The company ended up making Leslie an offer she couldn't refuse. She could keep her full-time job, work from home remotely, and travel back to Detroit for in-person meetings one week per month. So, Leslie ended up getting what she wanted, even though this unique work situation had never existed in the company before.

Leslie repeated something I had heard from every meditator I spoke with. She said, "The logical mind wants to listen to all the negative messages that tell you that you can't make it, you can't change jobs, you can't sell your house, you can't go into business for yourself. The clarity that comes from meditation puts you in touch with the deeper self. That deeper self, whatever you want to call it, when you let it know what you really want in life, it can make miraculous things happen. It is an inner-knowing that meditation gives you."

Despite meditation making life easier in many ways, we all go through trying times. In fact, everyone that I talked to for this book went through a major crisis in the past year or two, and they relied heavily on meditation to help pull them through.

In the middle of Leslie's move from Detroit, her mother died. Leslie spent time caring for her mother and was with her when she passed away. Leslie told me, "The centeredness and emotional stability that you get from meditation is a powerful tool when dealing with people who are sick or dying. You become very stable for the people around you."

Jackie, who I mentioned earlier, was in the process of changing jobs when she received a phone call that her five-year-old niece had a brain tumor and had been given only four to six weeks to live.

"When I got off the phone," Jackie told me, "I thought I was going to be a wreck. But, I stopped and I did my yoga and meditation, and I was fine. I just remember saying, 'I'm going to do this. I'm going to focus on this for a while and do my practice.' And in the middle of it, I remember this wave coming over me— this wave of calmness. It just settled everything down. It brought my emotions under control."

Michael, the CEO of the software business that shared his story earlier in this book, has a parent who is going through the final transition. Michael told me, "I've been able to spend time with my mom and really be with her—not thinking about the conference call I should be on, or about some email that I need to send. When I'm with her, I'm with her completely. During this time with my mom, the meditation has helped me deal with the fact that she is dying. In the past, I would have reached for chemicals in order to deal with the stress. But with meditation, I'm steady through the whole thing. And, I've been able to put all the walls down and give my heart to my mother."

Michael added, "I've been so grateful that my mother has been able to see me as this kind of person, instead of the one I was. And I feel now how our relationship should have been all the time."

I, too, have gone through a similar experience with the death of my father. I responded to dozens of false alarms in the middle of the night, and the calmness that resulted from my yoga and meditation allowed me to handle every situation and offer comfort to my parents.

There are infinite possibilities for the meditative mind. One meditating person can change the culture of a business. One meditating person can affect an entire community. Groups of meditating people can change the mind-set of an entire country. And as Sadhguru has often promised, if just one percent of the population becomes meditative, we can change the entire world and transform it into the kind of place we all truly want it to be. It is my hope that you'll join us in that effort.

Appendix

For information about Sadhguru, his humanitarian relief projects, and Project Bloom, visit the following:

* Isha Foundation – www.ishafoundation.org
* Inner Engineering Online – www.innerengineering.com
* Isha Kriya – www.ishakriya.com
* Project Bloom – www.projectbloom.com
* Sadhguru Videos – www.sadhguruvideos.com
* Project GreenHands – www.projectgreenhands.org
* Action for Rural Rejuvenation – www.ruralrejuvenation.org
* Isha Vidhya – www.ishavidhya.org
* Sadhguru on Twitter – @Jaggi_Vasudev
* Project Bloom on Twitter – @ishabloom
* Isha Foundation on Facebook – www.facebook.com/ishausa
* YouTube – www.youtube.com/ishafoundation

If you are interested in having someone speak to your business about organizing your own Project Bloom or running an Isha Kriya meditation workshop, send an email to bloom@projectbloom.com.

For more information about Sadhguru's yoga center in the mountains of Tennessee, the Isha Institute of Inner-sciences, call 931-668-1900 or visit www.IshaUSA.com or Isha Institute of Inner-sciences on Facebook.

Sadhguru's Inner Engineering course is available online at www.innerengineering.com. Upon registering for the online course, enter the code PW2000GJ for a $15 discount. After completing the course, you have an opportunity to attend an in-person program where you will learn a 21-minute meditation.

Acknowledgements

I appreciate the encouragement and support from many people who helped in bringing this book to print. I'd like to offer special recognition to Jennifer Wauson, my wife, who introduced me to yoga, and who allowed me to share the most intimate details of our life together in this book.

I would also like to thank Suzanne Boeters, Sadhguru's personal assistant, who was one of the first readers of this book, and found the time in Sadhguru's schedule for him to review it and give permission for it to be published.

I must also thank Darlene Wade for urging me to write this story and for supporting the efforts of Project Bloom.

In addition, special thanks go to Michael Gremley, Jackie Fitzgerald, and Leslie Crespi for sharing their stories about the impact meditation has had on their lives, and to Bob Brueck and MB Wilwau for the impact they have had on my life.

Special thanks and gratitude also go to Sadhguru, who taught me yoga and meditation and, in the process, gave me the tools to bloom.

Sadhguru Jaggi Vasudev
Founder, Isha Foundation